• INSTALL ELECTRICAL BREAKERS FOR ENTIRE SHOP WITHIN EASY REACH, CIRCUIT-RATED FOR SUFFICIENT AMPERAGE

• STOCK FIRST AID KIT WITH MATERIALS TO TREAT CUTS, GASHES, SPLINTERS, FOREIGN OBJECTS AND CHEMICALS IN EYES, AND BURNS

• HAVE TELEPHONE IN SHOP TO CALL FOR HELP

• INSTALL FIRE EXTINGUISHER RATED FOR A-, B-, AND C-CLASS FIRES

• WEAR EYE PROTECTION AT ALL TIMES

• LOCK CABINETS AND POWER TOOLS TO PROTECT CHILDREN AND INEXPERIENCED VISITORS

• USE DUST COLLECTOR TO KEEP SHOP DUST AT A MINIMUM

• WEAR SHIRT SLEEVES ABOVE ELBOWS

• WEAR CLOSE-FITTING CLOTHES

• WEAR LONG PANTS

• REMOVE WATCHES, RINGS, OR JEWELRY

• KEEP TABLE AND FENCE SURFACES WAXED AND RUST-FREE

• WEAR THICK-SOLED SHOES, PREFERABLY WITH STEEL TOES

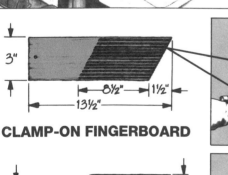

3"
8½" 1½"
13½"

CLAMP-ON FINGERBOARD

1½"
6" 2" 5" 1½"
3"
14½"

HAND-HELD FINGERBOARD

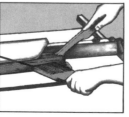

PROTECTION

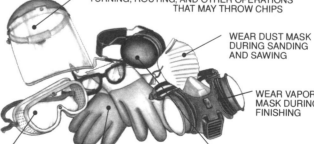

WEAR FULL FACE SHIELD DURING LATHE TURNING, ROUTING, AND OTHER OPERATIONS THAT MAY THROW CHIPS

WEAR DUST MASK DURING SANDING AND SAWING

WEAR VAPOR MASK DURING FINISHING

WEAR EAR PROTECTORS DURING ROUTING, PLANING, AND LONG, CONTINUOUS POWER TOOL OPERATION

WEAR RUBBER GLOVES FOR HANDLING DANGEROUS CHEMICALS

WEAR SAFETY GLASSES OR GOGGLES AT ALL TIMES

THE WORKSHOP COMPANION®

COMPLETE INDEX & SHOP MANUAL

TECHNIQUES FOR BETTER WOODWORKING

by Nick Engler

Rodale Press
Emmaus, Pennsylvania

If you have any questions or comments concerning this book, please write:
    Rodale Press
    Book Readers' Service
    33 East Minor Street
    Emmaus, PA 18098

About the Workshop Companion series: This series is written by Nick Engler, an experienced woodworker, writer, teacher, and inventor. He worked as a luthier for many years, making traditional American musical instruments before he founded *Hands On!* magazine. He has taught at the University of Cincinnati and gives woodworking seminars around the country. He contributes to woodworking magazines and designs tools for America's Best Tool Company. With the climax of this series, he has written 47 books.

Series Editor: Kevin Ireland
Editor: Tony O'Malley
Copy Editor: Sarah Dunn
Graphic Designers: Linda Watts and Marta Mitchell Strait
Graphic Artists: Mary Jane Favorite and Chris Walendzak
Master Craftsman: Jim McCann
Photographers: Karen Callahan and Mitch Mandel
Cover Photographer: Mitch Mandel
Index Compiler: Susan Nickol
Interior and endpaper illustrations by Mary Jane Favorite

ISBN 0–87596–739–6

4 6 8 10 9 7 5 3   hardcover

Patent Notice
Many of the jigs and fixtures shown in this book are patented, patent pending, or include patented features. Readers are encouraged to make a single copy of each for their personal use or for a gift. However, manufacture for sale or profit is forbidden without the written permission of the patent owner, America's Best Tool Company, Inc.

CONTENTS

REFERENCE CHARTS—CONTINUED

THE WORKSHOP COMPANION SERIES   120

INTRODUCTION

SCRAPS

Once a month I get together with a couple dozen craftsmen. We hijack a nearby restaurant and, like crusty fishermen, tell each other shop lies for a few hours. Often, the topic of prevarication turns to "rediscovered treasures"—bits of exotic wood, forgotten tools, and unfinished projects that woodworkers find when they clean out the bins, cabinets, and corners in their shops. Noncraftsmen might find this dull, but woodworkers are easily entertained. I have seen a woodworker describe the newly uncovered flotsam and jetsam at the bottom of his scrap bin to a spellbound audience for the better part of an hour. It was as if he were Cortez, returned from the New World with fantastic tales of Aztec gold.

I have that same pleasant feeling of rediscovery looking over my research notes for the 20 books in the **Workshop Companion** series. In many ways, these form a scrap bin of woodworking ideas—folder after folder of information that I have collected on the woodworking process, from lumbering to finishing and everything in between. And even though I've written extensively about this material, I enjoy going over it again, refreshing my memory and becoming reacquainted with interesting ideas, techniques, jigs, and

projects. As much as I love this stuff, I can't keep it all in my head. Most woodworkers, after all, can't rattle off the contents of their scrap bins, even though they seem to have an emotional bond with each and every board. There's just too much good stuff to keep track of.

You probably have a similar feeling about your woodworking library. Why else do we craftsmen save every single woodworking magazine we buy? Scraps of information, like scraps of wood, have exciting potential. A single board with just the right grain pattern often makes the difference between a good effort and a masterpiece. And so every board, no matter how small, is worth its weight in gold if you save it for just the right project. By the same token, a single tip or technique can often make a real difference in your craftsmanship. The trick is being able to ferret out those scraps of wood and information when they'll do you the most good.

I can help with *some* of that. I've yet to discover a good way to organize scrap wood—my boards always seems to dissolve into creative chaos within a few minutes of sorting them out. But I can make some of the valuable information in your library more accessible.

Whether you've collected all of the **Workshop Companion** books or just a few, you have a ton of information to sort through. Each book contains diverse material on a single woodworking topic, and the entire series includes over 2,500 pages of information, making it one of the largest and most comprehensive works on woodworking ever published. To help you find those elusive scraps of information when you need them, we've put together a comprehensive guide and cross-reference to the **Workshop Companion** series.

The **Complete Index and Shop Manual** actually contains four distinct parts, each designed to help you find a specific kind of information quickly. The **Comprehensive Index** includes every topic in the series, as the name suggests. There are also separate indices for the **Jigs and Fixtures** and the **Projects** from the series, so you can quickly find exactly what you want in these areas. In the last section— **Reference Charts**—I've collected information that most woodworkers use on a daily basis into a single, convenient location. If all you need is a quick read or something to jog your memory, you'll likely find it in one of these charts.

How to Use This Book

This index is like any shop tool—you need to know how to use it in order to get a specific job done. Here's how the *Workshop Companion Complete Index and Shop Manual* works.

First, each section is organized alphabetically. To the right of each entry is a two- or three-letter code that indicates the book in which you'll find information on that entry. A key at the bottom of each page provides the corresponding titles of all the volumes in the *Workshop Companion* series.

Second, because a picture really can be worth a thousand words, we've included photos wherever possible—every project is shown, every jig and fixture, and just to make the index more fun to use, a few photos or illustrations are displayed on every page of the comprehensive index. It's worth noting that in many cases, the photo of a jig is all you'll need to make your own version. In effect, the photo gives you the jig idea, and for many craftsmen, making the jig is easy once they've seen the concept.

Before I go, I'd like to thank you sincerely for choosing the *Workshop Companion* books to be part of your library. I realize that many of these tomes will be used in your shops and dens for years to come, and this is an honor that I did not take lightly when I wrote them. As one craftsman to another, I know just how precious these scraps of information can be.

With all good wishes,

P.S. If you'd like to order any of the books in the *Workshop Companion* series, you'll find a brief description of each volume along with a toll-free telephone number on pages 120–121.

COMPREHENSIVE INDEX

COMPREHENSIVE INDEX

Note: Page numbers are preceded by initials indicating which book the references are found in. The shaded key below lists each book with its initials.

A

Abrasive belt and disc cleaner

KEY: AR—Advanced Routing; **BC**—Making Boxes and Chests; **BIC**—Making Built-In Cabinets; **BS**—Using the Band Saw; **DB**—Making Desks and Bookcases; **DP**—Using the Drill Press; **F**—Finishing; **FC**—Finish Carpentry; **GC**—Gluing and Clamping; **HT**—Using Hand Tools; **JF**—Making Jigs and Fixtures;

Shaping a chair seat with an adze

Air scrubber traps sanding dust

Banding inlaid in a panel

B

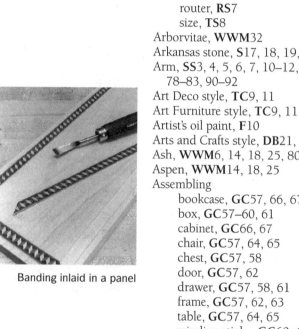

KEY: AR—Advanced Routing; **BC**—Making Boxes and Chests; **BIC**—Making Built-In Cabinets; **BS**—Using the Band Saw;
DB—Making Desks and Bookcases; **DP**—Using the Drill Press; **F**—Finishing; **FC**—Finish Carpentry;
GC—Gluing and Clamping; **HT**—Using Hand Tools; **JF**—Making Jigs and Fixtures;

Kerf bending

Biscuit joint

Blade stabilizers

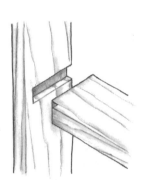

Blind dado joint

Lathe-turned box

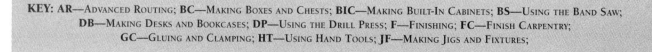

C

Buffing head

Bullnose plane trimming a rabbet

Cabinet scraper

Clamping cauls protect
workpiece

Center finder

Dowel centers

KEY: AR—Advanced Routing; **BC**—Making Boxes and Chests; **BIC**—Making Built-In Cabinets; **BS**—Using the Band Saw;
DB—Making Desks and Bookcases; **DP**—Using the Drill Press; **F**—Finishing; **FC**—Finish Carpentry;
GC—Gluing and Clamping; **HT**—Using Hand Tools; **JF**—Making Jigs and Fixtures;

Windsor chair

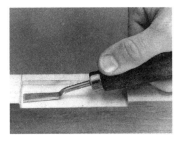

Dog leg chisel trimming a hinge mortise

Clamping with pinch dogs

Spring clamps

Rub collars

Contractor's saw

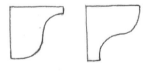
KEY: AR—Advanced Routing; **BC**—Making Boxes and Chests; **BIC**—Making Built-In Cabinets; **BS**—Using the Band Saw;
DB—Making Desks and Bookcases; **DP**—Using the Drill Press; **F**—Finishing; **FC**—Finish Carpentry;
GC—Gluing and Clamping; **HT**—Using Hand Tools; **JF**—Making Jigs and Fixtures;

Dadoing insert

Queen Anne–style slant-
front desk

Detail sander reaches all the
way into corners

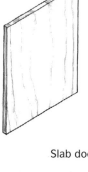

Slab door

Board-and-batten door

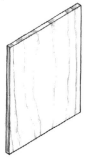

Frame-and-panel door

Doweling jig

Joist brace

Forstner bit *(left)*
Multi-spur bit *(right)*

Drilling a screw pocket

KEY: AR—Advanced Routing; **BC**—Making Boxes and Chests; **BIC**—Making Built-In Cabinets; **BS**—Using the Band Saw;
DB—Making Desks and Bookcases; **DP**—Using the Drill Press; **F**—Finishing; **FC**—Finish Carpentry;
GC—Gluing and Clamping; **HT**—Using Hand Tools; **JF**—Making Jigs and Fixtures;

Drum sanding on the drill press

American Empire style

European-style hinge

File card

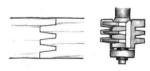

Finger glue joint

KEY: AR—Advanced Routing; **BC**—Making Boxes and Chests; **BIC**—Making Built-In Cabinets; **BS**—Using the Band Saw;
DB—Making Desks and Bookcases; **DP**—Using the Drill Press; **F**—Finishing; **FC**—Finish Carpentry;
GC—Gluing and Clamping; **HT**—Using Hand Tools; **JF**—Making Jigs and Fixtures;

Flexible curves

French curves

Fretwork, **SS**2, 3, 24, 25, 53, 54, 55, 100–107
Fruitwood, **WWM**27
Fuming, **F**56, 121
Furniture traditions, **TC**8, 9, 10

G

Gaps, **F**33, 34, 36
Garnet, **SP**42, 43, 44, 58
Gauges
    combination, **HT**115–121
    contour, **HT**20
    cutting, **HT**17, 18, 115, 117–121
    depth, **HT**7, 8, 10
    marking, **HT**8, 17, 18, 41, 49, 115, 117, 120, 121
    mortising, **HT**17, 18, 115, 117–121
    profile, **HT**20
Gel stain, **F**10, 58
German-style workbench, **WSF**17
Gervenius, **TS**2
Gingerbread, **SS**54, 55
Glaze
    finish stain, **F**60, 106
    rubbing compound, **F**86, 87
Gloss, high, **F**86, 87, 88
Gloves, rubber, **F**18
Glue, **F**33
    adhesive, **GC**3
    aliphatic resin, **GC**4, 6, 7, 11, 14
    applications, **GC**8–10, 14
    bottle, **GC**42
    carpenter's, **GC**7
    caulk/sealer, **GC**10, 14
    ceramic and glass adhesive, **GC**10
    choosing, **GC**11, 12, 14, 15
    classification, **GC**12, 14
    cohesion, **GC**3
    comparing, **GC**11
    contact cement, **GC**6, 10, 11, 14, 17, 42, 74, 78–80, 81, 82
    craft adhesive, **GC**10
    curing, **GC**3, 5, 8, 15, 17, 35, 40, 45, 81
    cyanoacrylate, **GC**6, 8, 11, 14, 17, 19, 42
    elastomer adhesive, **GC**9, 10
    epoxy cement, **GC**4, 6, 9, 12, 14, 17, 30, 36, 42, 44, 46
    gun, **GC**10, 15

    hide, **GC**6, 7, 11, 14, 80, 81
    hot-melt, **GC**6, 10, 11, 14, 19, 80, 81
    ingredients, **GC**5–10
    mastic, **GC**6, 9, 14
    model cement, **GC**4
    one-part, **GC**6
    panel adhesive, **GC**6
    plastic resin, **GC**6, 8, 14
    polymerization, **GC**5
    polyvinyl resin, **GC**4–6, 7, 14
    pot, **GC**6, 7
    properties, **GC**5–9, 11, 12, 14, 15, 35, 37, 40, 41, 45, 46
    resorcinol, **GC**6, 9, 14, 36
    safety, **GC**8, 15, 35, 41, 45
    sheets, **GC**80, 81
    silicone caulk, **GC**9, 10, 14
    spreader, **GC**42
    Super Glue, **GC**6, 8, 14
    thermoplastic, **GC**10
    two-part, **GC**9
    type, **GC**6, 14
    urea-formaldehyde, **GC**6, 8, 14
    water-based, **GC**4, 5, 10, 11, 41, 43, 45, 46, 79
    white, **GC**4–6, 7, 14, 36, 41, 42, 60
    yellow, **GC**4, 6, 7, 14, 36, 41, 42, 60
Glue block, **BC**59, 92, 93; **JW**49–50
Glue joint, **AR**27; **BC**93; **RS**71, 73
    adherends, **GC**3
    adhesion, **GC**3
    cleavage, **GC**3
    cohesion, **GC**3
    comparing glues, **GC**11
    gaps, **GC**4
    interphase, **GC**3, 42
    joinery, **GC**51
    peeling, **GC**3
    pressure, **GC**17, 18
    shear, **GC**3
    stains, **GC**43, 46
    starved joint, **GC**17, 38, 46
    strength, **GC**3–6, 37, 39, 40, 66
    stress, **GC**3, 5, 38
    tension, **GC**3
Glue properties
    chemical resistance, **GC**6
    clamp time, **GC**5
    closed assembly time, **GC**5, 8, 9, 15, 40
    cost, **GC**6, 14
    creep, **GC**5, 46

Countour gauge transfers molding profiles

Hide glue heated in a double boiler

Hot-melt glue gun

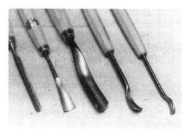

Assorted carving gouges

Gouge slip

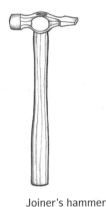

Joiner's hammer

Hand scraper

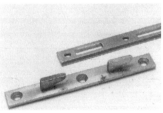

Bed rail fasteners

KEY: AR—Advanced Routing; **BC**—Making Boxes and Chests; **BIC**—Making Built-In Cabinets; **BS**—Using the Band Saw;
DB—Making Desks and Bookcases; **DP**—Using the Drill Press; **F**—Finishing; **FC**—Finish Carpentry;
GC—Gluing and Clamping; **HT**—Using Hand Tools; **JF**—Making Jigs and Fixtures;

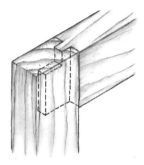

Haunched mortise-and-tenon joint

Honing guides

An inshave carves concave shapes

Intarsia

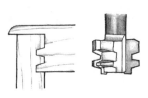

Drawer lock joint

Round mortise-and-tenon joint

Combination jointer/planer machine

Jointing end grain

Face jointing with push
blocks

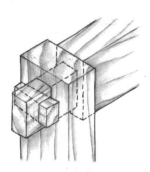

Keyed mortise-and-tenon
joint

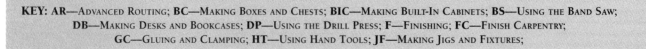

L

Polishing with a lamb's wool bonnet

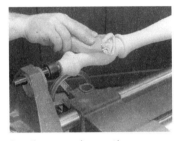

Sanding a turning on the lathe

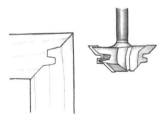

Locked miter joint

JW—Joining Wood; **RS**—Routing and Shaping; **S**—Sharpening; **SP**—Sanding and Planing; **SS**—Using the Scroll Saw;
TC—Making Tables and Chairs; **TS**—Using the Table Saw; **WSF**—Workbenches and Shop Furniture;
WWM—Wood and Woodworking Materials

Dead-blow mallet

M

Marquetry inlay patches

KEY: AR—Advanced Routing; **BC**—Making Boxes and Chests; **BIC**—Making Built-In Cabinets; **BS**—Using the Band Saw;
DB—Making Desks and Bookcases; **DP**—Using the Drill Press; **F**—Finishing; **FC**—Finish Carpentry;
GC—Gluing and Clamping; **HT**—Using Hand Tools; **JF**—Making Jigs and Fixtures;

Compound miter cut on the table saw

Using a miter gauge on a router table

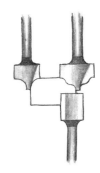

Molding made from multiple router bits

Molding head cutter on the table saw

Mortising with the drill press

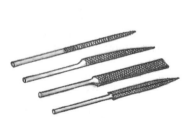

Needle files

Overhead blade guard

Patternmaker's vise

Compass plane adjusts for concave and convex shapes

Shoulder plane

Side-rabbet plane trims the vertical walls of dadoes and rabbets

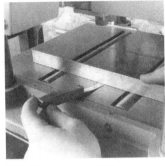

Checking planer roller height

Plug cutter

Laying out angles with a
protractor head

Radial drill press

Pivot fence for resawing

Rotary rasps

Smoothing a dado bottom with a router plane

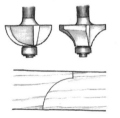

Rule joint

S

Countour sanders

Japanese dozuki saw

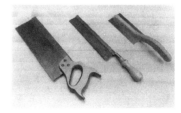

Tenon saw *(left)*, dovetail saw *(middle)*, and flush-cutting saw *(right)*

JW—J̲o̲i̲n̲i̲n̲g̲ ̲W̲o̲o̲d̲; **RS**—R̲o̲u̲t̲i̲n̲g̲ ̲a̲n̲d̲ ̲S̲h̲a̲p̲i̲n̲g̲; **S**—S̲h̲a̲r̲p̲e̲n̲i̲n̲g̲; **SP**—S̲a̲n̲d̲i̲n̲g̲ ̲a̲n̲d̲ ̲P̲l̲a̲n̲i̲n̲g̲; **SS**—U̲s̲i̲n̲g̲ ̲t̲h̲e̲ ̲S̲c̲r̲o̲l̲l̲ ̲S̲a̲w̲;
TC—M̲a̲k̲i̲n̲g̲ ̲T̲a̲b̲l̲e̲s̲ ̲a̲n̲d̲ ̲C̲h̲a̲i̲r̲s̲; **TS**—U̲s̲i̲n̲g̲ ̲t̲h̲e̲ ̲T̲a̲b̲l̲e̲ ̲S̲a̲w̲; **WSF**—W̲o̲r̲k̲b̲e̲n̲c̲h̲e̲s̲ ̲a̲n̲d̲ ̲S̲h̲o̲p̲ ̲F̲u̲r̲n̲i̲t̲u̲r̲e̲;
WWM—W̲o̲o̲d̲ ̲a̲n̲d̲ ̲W̲o̲o̲d̲w̲o̲r̲k̲i̲n̲g̲ ̲M̲a̲t̲e̲r̲i̲a̲l̲s̲

Scorp, used for hollowing
concave shapes

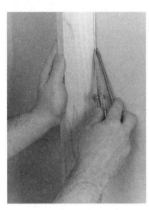

Marking a scribe strip
with a compass

KEY: AR—Advanced Routing; **BC**—Making Boxes and Chests; **BIC**—Making Built-In Cabinets; **BS**—Using the Band Saw;
DB—Making Desks and Bookcases; **DP**—Using the Drill Press; **F**—Finishing; **FC**—Finish Carpentry;
GC—Gluing and Clamping; **HT**—Using Hand Tools; **JF**—Making Jigs and Fixtures;

Shaker style table and chair

Shavehook with interchangeable blades

Traditional shaving horse

Sliding dovetail joint

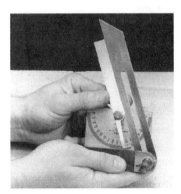

Sliding T-bevel transfers angles from protractor to workpiece

Split tenons

Spokeshave shaping a cabriole leg

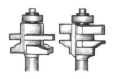
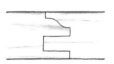

Stile-and-rail joint

JW—Joining Wood; **RS**—Routing and Shaping; **S**—Sharpening; **SP**—Sanding and Planing; **SS**—Using the Scroll Saw;
TC—Making Tables and Chairs; **TS**—Using the Table Saw; **WSF**—Workbenches and Shop Furniture;
WWM—Wood and Woodworking Materials

Strip sander

Surform rasp

KEY: AR—Advanced Routing; **BC**—Making Boxes and Chests; **BIC**—Making Built-In Cabinets; **BS**—Using the Band Saw;
DB—Making Desks and Bookcases; **DP**—Using the Drill Press; **F**—Finishing; **FC**—Finish Carpentry;
GC—Gluing and Clamping; **HT**—Using Hand Tools; **JF**—Making Jigs and Fixtures;

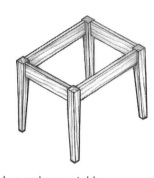

Leg-and-apron table construction

Poringer table

Trestle table construction

Tail vise

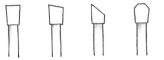

Pattern routing technique

Common table saw teeth profiles *(left to right):* flat or raker, bevel, steep bevel, and triple chip

Testing flatness of
table saw

Toggle clamp

Tongue-and-groove joint

KEY: AR—Advanced Routing; **BC**—Making Boxes and Chests; **BIC**—Making Built-In Cabinets; **BS**—Using the Band Saw;
DB—Making Desks and Bookcases; **DP**—Using the Drill Press; **F**—Finishing; **FC**—Finish Carpentry;
GC—Gluing and Clamping; **HT**—Using Hand Tools; **JF**—Making Jigs and Fixtures;

U

Drawing a circle with trammel points

A Tucker Vise swivels 360°

JW—Joining Wood; **RS**—Routing and Shaping; **S**—Sharpening; **SP**—Sanding and Planing; **SS**—Using the Scroll Saw;
TC—Making Tables and Chairs; **TS**—Using the Table Saw; **WSF**—Workbenches and Shop Furniture;
WWM—Wood and Woodworking Materials

Veneer pins and veneer tape

Veneer saw

KEY: AR—Advanced Routing; **BC**—Making Boxes and Chests; **BIC**—Making Built-In Cabinets; **BS**—Using the Band Saw;
DB—Making Desks and Bookcases; **DP**—Using the Drill Press; **F**—Finishing; **FC**—Finish Carpentry;
GC—Gluing and Clamping; **HT**—Using Hand Tools; **JF**—Making Jigs and Fixtures;

Wet grinder

Winding sticks measure flatness

Wire wheel

Wobble dado blade

Wooden hinge

Modern cabinetmaker's workbench

X

Y

Z

Workmate

Zero-clearance table
insert

KEY: AR—Advanced Routing; **BC**—Making Boxes and Chests; **BIC**—Making Built-In Cabinets; **BS**—Using the Band Saw;
DB—Making Desks and Bookcases; **DP**—Using the Drill Press; **F**—Finishing; **FC**—Finish Carpentry;
GC—Gluing and Clamping; **HT**—Using Hand Tools; **JF**—Making Jigs and Fixtures;
JW—Joining Wood; **RS**—Routing and Shaping; **S**—Sharpening; **SP**—Sanding and Planing;
SS—Using the Scroll Saw; **TC**—Making Tables and Chairs; **TS**—Using the Table Saw;
WSF—Workbenches and Shop Furniture; **WWM**—Wood and Woodworking Materials

PROJECT INDEX

PROJECTS

are the best part of woodworking. Once you've learned a new technique, there's nothing more rewarding than putting it to the test in a well-made project. This index includes 51 projects that are sure to put your new skills to good use.

Note: Page numbers are preceded by initials indicating which book the references are found in. The shaded key below lists each book with its initials.

ADJUSTABLE BOOKSHELVES

This bookcase has a dowelled face frame concealing a basic case made with dado joints. Four design variations accompany the plan (Mission, Queen Anne, Victorian, and Southwest style).

DB104–109

ADJUSTABLE SHOP STOOL

This stool can be adjusted to heights from 16 to 27 inches. A tool bin beneath adjusts independently.

WSF117–121

APOTHECARY HIGHBOY

Organize a houseful of small objects in this storage chest. Mortise-and-tenons join the lower case, while the top and drawers are all joined with dadoes.

BC104–117

BOW-FRONT SOFA TABLE

The gently bowed front apron on this sofa table has a dramatic effect, but it is easy to make using a simple kerf-bending technique. The rest of the table employs traditional joinery.

TS116

BROKEN HEART BOX

This project is more of a puzzle than a box for storage. The pieces slide apart only when moved in exactly the right order.

BC118–122

BUTLER'S TABLE

With its four leaves opened flat, this oval coffee table has no sharp edges or corners to bump your knees. With the leaves folded up, the detachable top can be used as a large serving tray.

F114–121

CABINETMAKER'S WORKBENCH

This sturdy workbench has a solid maple top, an open shelf under the top that's accessible from all sides, and plenty of drawer and storage space in the cabinet.

JW111

COFFERED CEILING

Transform a plain room into an elegant one with this coffered ceiling. It's no more than a series of simple moldings applied in a grid.

FC84–94

CANDLESTAND

This Shaker-inspired table stands sturdily on three legs, no matter how uneven your floor. Sliding routed dovetails join the legs to the turned column.

RS112

COMPOUND-CUT CHESS SET

With the right technique, a band saw can be a sculptor's tool. All these chess pieces and the box-jointed board/storage container were cut on the band saw.

BS114

CAPE COD ROCKER

An American classic, this porch rocker can be built in any home shop using a lathe and a band saw. The long back posts are made in two segments, and the curved parts are resawn from thick stock.

TC104–115

CONTEMPORARY KEEPING CHEST

This 24 × 12-inch chest features geometrically patterned splines at the mitered corners, and the same pattern is inlaid into the top. Concealed hardware makes the exterior clean and crisp.

WWM76

CARPENTER'S TOTE

Plywood construction and heavy-duty hardware make this a long-lasting tool tote. It's a basic six-sided box with the lid cut off at an angle. Five drawers hold plenty of small tools.

BC80–85

CORNER CUPBOARD

Uncomplicated and well-proportioned, this corner cupboard has plenty of storage space but takes up only a small amount of floor space that otherwise might be wasted.

TS101

JW—Joining Wood; **RS**—Routing and Shaping; **S**—Sharpening; **SP**—Sanding and Planing; **SS**—Using the Scroll Saw; **TC**—Making Tables and Chairs; **TS**—Using the Table Saw; **WSF**—Workbenches and Shop Furniture; **WWM**—Wood and Woodworking Materials

COUNTRY LETTER DESK

There's plenty of drawer space and a storage bin below the hinged writing surface of this writing desk, which features tapered legs, pegged mortise-and-tenon joinery, and dovetails.

DB88

HAND TOOL CABINET

With its box-jointed case and raised-panel doors, this cabinet will display fine craftsmanship while keeping your valuable hand tools organized and safe.

WSF93

FRETWORK MIRROR

This mirror starts with a simple picture frame that is accented with easily cut borders of scroll-sawed fretwork.

SS100

HANGING DISPLAY CASE

Glass shelves and the mirrored back on this cabinet combine to make displayed items more visible than if on open shelves. The project features a face-frame case with mortise-and-tenon doors.

SS107

GRANDMOTHER CLOCK

This clock has all the features of a grandfather clock—scrolled bonnet, glass-doored pendulum case, mechanical works—but is more manageable in size.

WWM92

HERRINGBONE CUTTING BOARD

The ultimate project for using up "scrap" wood, this cutting board can be made using any variety of woods you have in your scrap bin.

WWM89

HALF-MOON BENCH

Dovetails and through-wedged tenons combine to form an indestructible bench from just four boards. The same design can be scaled down to make a step stool or scaled up for a table.

JW108

INSPIRED CHEST OF DRAWERS

Half-blind dovetailed drawers glide on web frames, which are dadoed into the solid case sides of this Shaker-inspired five-drawer chest.

BC86

KEY: **AR**—Advanced Routing; **BC**—Making Boxes and Chests; **BIC**—Making Built-In Cabinets; **BS**—Using the Band Saw; **DB**—Making Desks and Bookcases; **DP**—Using the Drill Press; **F**—Finishing; **FC**—Finish Carpentry; **GC**—Gluing and Clamping; **HT**—Using Hand Tools; **JF**—Making Jigs and Fixtures;

KEEPING BOX

The raised-panel lid and a drawer front that's disguised by box joints distinguish this project from an ordinary box.

BC96–103

LAP DESK

Organize your stationery, coupons, correspondence, and even your bills in this traditional lap desk. The box features a frame-and-panel top and three dadoed inner compartments.

DB110

KITCHEN CABINETS

Here's a complete kitchen project that shows you how to plan, build, and install every element, including countertops and sink.

BIC98

LOW-BACK CHAIR

This reproduction Shaker chair has a low back so it can slide under a dining table. All the parts and tenons are turned, except for the back slats, which are steam-bent.

TC92

KNIFE BLOCK
AND CUTTING BOARD

This knife block is cut from solid stock, then laminated. Compact and practical, this project can be made and finished in one day.

F107

MINIATURE CHEST

Once known as a "keeping box" utilized for storing valuable papers and jewelry, this 10-inch-tall chest features through-dovetail joinery at the box corners and mitered feet.

RS90

KNIFE CADDY

Use this lidded carryall for tools, sewing, or arts-and-crafts supplies—even to carry food to a picnic. The project's splayed corners are easy to cut using the blade and miter gauge angles that are provided.

TS110

MINIATURE CHEST
OF DRAWERS

Small things like jewelry, sewing notions, and collectibles need special housing. This chest is made with rabbet-and-dado joinery.

JW101

JW—Joining Wood; RS—Routing and Shaping; S—Sharpening; SP—Sanding and Planing; SS—Using the Scroll Saw; TC—Making Tables and Chairs; TS—Using the Table Saw; WSF—Workbenches and Shop Furniture; WWM—Wood and Woodworking Materials

MINIATURE MULE CHEST

Combining a lidded top section with a lower drawer ensures that even tiny items will be more accessible in this chest.

F92

NESTING BOXES

This set of boxes was band-sawed from a single block of glued-up stock. The trick is in the sequence of the cuts.

BS111

MISSION BOOKCASE

An American classic design, this bookcase features frame-and-panel sides and pegged through-mortise-and-tenon joinery. This project explains how to cut your stock so quarter-sawn oak shows on all prominent surfaces.

WWM103

NESTING TABLES

A simple space-saving design gives you three tables in the space of one. The parts are different in size, but the construction procedures are identical for all three tables.

TC116

MISSION OCCASIONAL TABLE

The round top on this knock-down table rests in dadoes cut into the legs. The stretchers are wedge-tenoned through the legs. This design can be easily modified for a matching coffee table.

DP113

NOAH'S BANDSAWED ARK

An exercise in careful cutting, this vessel and the animals surrounding it are made using the band saw and patterns supplied with the project.

BS92

MODULAR WORKBENCH

This heavy-duty bench is designed as three separate components—trestle frame, work surface, and top.

WSF105

PANELED DOOR

Making your own paneled doors allows you to use any species of wood. This project shows five styles, including glazed doors, all made with mortise-and-tenon joinery.

FC115

KEY: **AR**—ADVANCED ROUTING; **BC**—MAKING BOXES AND CHESTS; **BIC**—MAKING BUILT-IN CABINETS; **BS**—USING THE BAND SAW; **DB**—MAKING DESKS AND BOOKCASES; **DP**—USING THE DRILL PRESS; **F**—FINISHING; **FC**—FINISH CARPENTRY; **GC**—GLUING AND CLAMPING; **HT**—USING HAND TOOLS; **JF**—MAKING JIGS AND FIXTURES;

PEWTER RACK

A weekend project made with basic rabbet and stopped-dado joinery, this functional storage rack will hold dishes, silverware, or knickknacks.

JW96

ROUTED BOX

Using just a band saw and a router, you can make this box and fitted lid from solid wood. Choose square, round, or glued-up scraps of contrasting woods for your stock.

RS118

QUEEN ANNE SIDE TABLE

The cabriole legs on this table are a classic example of the challenging shapes you can cut with a band saw. The table also features dovetailed drawers and traditional mortise-and-tenon joinery.

BS104

SAWBUCK PICNIC TABLES AND BENCHES

The sawbuck design is exceptionally strong and versatile. Made from 2-by stock, both the benches and table are designed to fold flat for easy storage.

TC98

"ROUND AND ROUND" WHIRLIGIG

A horizontal "wind wheel" powers this whimsical creation, in which a woman chases a dog, which chases a cat, which chases a mouse, which chases the woman…

SS114

SNOWFLAKE BENCH AND TABLE

This furniture set is characterized by repeating wedge-shaped patterns cut with a band saw and then pattern-routed.

AR94

ROUND TAVERN TABLE

This table is an exercise in solid wood joinery and includes methods for selecting stock to ensure the tabletop stays flat. Rails are joined to tapered legs with pegged tenons.

WWM115

STAINED-GLASS AND CUT-GLASS WINDOWS

Though stained-glass and cut-glass windows are notorious for heat loss, you can make them function effectively in a home. The trick? Build an insulated window frame around the glass.

FC108

JW—Joining Wood; RS—Routing and Shaping; S—Sharpening; SP—Sanding and Planing; SS—Using the Scroll Saw; TC—Making Tables and Chairs; TS—Using the Table Saw; WSF—Workbenches and Shop Furniture; WWM—Wood and Woodworking Materials

STEP-BACK CUPBOARD

This traditional cupboard combines concealed storage, an open display shelf, and a counter-height work surface. The case is dadoed together, while the door frames are mortised and tenoned around flat panels.

F99

VICTORIAN DISPLAY SHELVES

Open fretwork sides support quarter-round shelves on this delicate corner unit.

SS107

STORAGE STAND

Use this mobile storage stand for almost any shop tool—jointer, sander, scroll saw, or whatever you have in your shop. You can adjust the proportions to make stands for other uses, like a sharpening station or tool cabinet.

WSF84

WOODEN PENS AND PENCILS

Two turned wooden cylinders and a pen or pencil hardware kit are all it takes to produce these beautiful writing instruments.

DP119

TIP-AND-TURN TABLE

A marriage of beauty and practicality, the oval top of this table can provide convenient dining for one or pivot to vertical so the table can be placed against a wall when not in use.

AR86

KEY: **AR**—ADVANCED ROUTING; **BC**—MAKING BOXES AND CHESTS; **BIC**—MAKING BUILT-IN CABINETS; **BS**—USING THE BAND SAW; **DB**—MAKING DESKS AND BOOKCASES; **DP**—USING THE DRILL PRESS; **F**—FINISHING; **FC**—FINISH CARPENTRY; **GC**—GLUING AND CLAMPING; **HT**—USING HAND TOOLS; **JF**—MAKING JIGS AND FIXTURES; **JW**—JOINING WOOD; **RS**—ROUTING AND SHAPING; **S**—SHARPENING; **SP**—SANDING AND PLANING; **SS**—USING THE SCROLL SAW; **TC**—MAKING TABLES AND CHAIRS; **TS**—USING THE TABLE SAW; **WSF**—WORKBENCHES AND SHOP FURNITURE; **WWM**—WOOD AND WOODWORKING MATERIALS

JIG AND FIXTURE INDEX

JIGS AND FIXTURES

make woodworking safer and easier, and thus a lot more fun. With the right jig or fixture, you can double or triple the number of jobs a particular tool can do. This index includes over 200 jigs, fixtures, tools, and shop storage devices, each one designed to expand your woodworking horizons.

Note: Page numbers are preceded by initials indicating which book the references are found in. The shaded key below lists each book with its initials.

BAND CLAMP PEG RAIL

When you need a band clamp, the last thing you want is to have to untangle it. This rack consists of a mounting plate and two dowels that will keep your band clamps tangle-free.

GC31

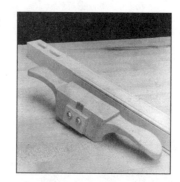

BEADING TOOL

Designed to use commercial cutters, this beading tool is for cutting fine decorative moldings and trim.

HT98

BAND SAW AUXILIARY TABLE

Cut much larger pieces of stock more easily with this band saw extension table.

BS47

BENCH DOGS

Make your own bench dogs, either square or round, from a dense hardwood like maple or beech. The ones shown here use simple bullet catches instead of steel springs to hold the dog at the desired height.

WSF43

BAND SAW SPEED CHANGER

The step pulleys in this fixture let you add variable speed to your band saw so you can match blade speed to the material you're cutting.

BS20

BENCH HOOK

A bench hook lets you hold a workpiece securely for hand sawing. The work rests against the rear stop, while the front stop rests against the bench edge.

WSF47; see also HT28

KEY: AR—ADVANCED ROUTING; BC—MAKING BOXES AND CHESTS; BIC—MAKING BUILT-IN CABINETS; BS—USING THE BAND SAW; DB—MAKING DESKS AND BOOKCASES; DP—USING THE DRILL PRESS; F—FINISHING; FC—FINISH CARPENTRY; GC—GLUING AND CLAMPING; HT—USING HAND TOOLS; JF—MAKING JIGS AND FIXTURES;

BENCH STOPS

Bench stops keep a workpiece from moving around on your bench. This one spans the entire width of the bench.

WSF39

C-CLAMP, LONG-REACH

This clamp reaches 7 inches in from the edge of an assembly, making it great for applying pressure to a veneer repair or correcting a mis-aligned joint.

GC119; see also JF49, 53

BISCUIT JOINT ROUTING TEMPLATE

With a slot-cutting bit in your router and this template, you can make precise biscuit joints without a biscuit-jointing machine.

RS69

C-CLAMP HOLDER

C-clamps are often-used tools that seem always to be misplaced. This rack gives all your C-clamps a home, with adjustable hanging pegs for any size clamps.

GC32

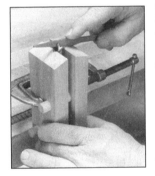

BRAD-POINT BIT SHARPENING JIG

File your own brad-point bits with this jig. It holds the bit securely and has angled bearing surfaces for filing the point and spurs of the bit. A thumbscrew raises the bit incrementally in the jig.

S81; see also DP45

CALIPER, FIXED

Turn round tenons of consistent diameter with this fixed caliper. A drilled hole represents the actual mortise size, while a stepped gauge warns you when you're close to the final size.

JW77; see also DP77, JF40, TC72

BREAST BIB

This jig lets you lean into your drilling when using a bit and brace. The added body pressure makes for efficient and more accurate drilling.

HT57

CAM CLAMP

Similar to quick-action bar clamps, the heads on these cam clamps move just $\frac{1}{4}$ inch when you throw the cam, enough for many kinds of light-pressure glue-ups.

GC99; see also JF51

JW—Joining Wood; **RS**—Routing and Shaping; **S**—Sharpening; **SP**—Sanding and Planing; **SS**—Using the Scroll Saw; **TC**—Making Tables and Chairs; **TS**—Using the Table Saw; **WSF**—Workbenches and Shop Furniture; **WWM**—Wood and Woodworking Materials

CASTERS, RETRACTABLE

Putting a tool or cabinet on wheels is great until you want it to stay still. This design for retractable casters lets you have it both ways. All it takes is a hinged block, a pivoting cam, and a hook-and-eye.

WSF64

CHISEL BIT/ CHUCK CLAMP

Use this flat chisel bit and the leverage from your drill press to true up the sides and ends of drilled-out mortises. The clamp prevents the chuck from turning.

DP74

CENTER FINDER

Three small strips of wood are all that's needed to make this useful tool for finding the center point of cylinders and small, round parts.

HT19

CHISEL GUIDE

This jig will help you true up the sides and ends of a drilled-out mortise. It's held in a vise along with the workpiece and adjusts for different size stock.

DP71

CHAIR LEG DRILL GUIDE

This plywood jig guides your drill for making compound angled mortises where chair legs meet the seat bottom.

TC77

CHISEL PLANE JIG

Turn any chisel into a chisel plane with this jig. It's great for trimming corners on tenon cheeks and rabbets and for cleaning glue from case joints.

HT44

CHAIR POST ROUTING JIG

This jig holds a chair's back post at the slight angle needed for routing the rail mortises.

TC62

CHISEL RACK

This box keeps chisels organized and their edges protected. It has a base for free-standing use.

HT76

KEY: AR—ADVANCED ROUTING; **BC**—MAKING BOXES AND CHESTS; **BIC**—MAKING BUILT-IN CABINETS; **BS**—USING THE BAND SAW;
DB—MAKING DESKS AND BOOKCASES; **DP**—USING THE DRILL PRESS; **F**—FINISHING; **FC**—FINISH CARPENTRY;
GC—GLUING AND CLAMPING; **HT**—USING HAND TOOLS; **JF**—MAKING JIGS AND FIXTURES;

CIRCLE-CUTTING JIG FOR THE BAND SAW

Made from just two pieces of scrap wood, this L-shaped jig lets you cut perfect circles on the band saw.

BS84

CIRCULAR SAW GUIDE

This straightedge fence jig saves you from measuring the blade-to-fence offset every time you cut plywood and other sheet goods.

BIC46; see also JF117, FC38

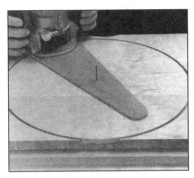

CIRCLE-CUTTING ROUTER SOLE

Rout perfect circles with this elongated router sole. It replaces your router's sole plate and attaches in seconds.

RS39; see also AR42

CLAMPING GRID

This grid provides a perfectly flat surface for all kinds of glue-ups. The feet can be located anywhere on the grid so they'll never be in the way.

GC69

CIRCLE-ROUTING JIG

Rout circles with a 6- to 24-inch radius using this jig. The separate pivot assembly is designed so you don't have to drill a hole in the work-piece.

TC49

CLAMPING PRESS

This press works in two directions—downward, like a conventional veneer press, and sideways, for gluing stock edge to edge.

GC111

CIRCLE-ROUTING SLIDING TABLE

With this auxiliary sliding table jig, you can precisely rout circles as small as 3 inches in diameter on your router table.

RS39; see also AR41

COMBINATION GAUGE

Here's a tool that combines a marking gauge, a cutting gauge, and two mortising gauges. They function independently so you can keep multiple settings when laying out any joint.

HT115

JW—Joining Wood; RS—Routing and Shaping; S—Sharpening; SP—Sanding and Planing; SS—Using the Scroll Saw; TC—Making Tables and Chairs; TS—Using the Table Saw; WSF—Workbenches and Shop Furniture; WWM—Wood and Woodworking Materials

COPING JIG

Moldings that are installed at an angle to the wall and ceiling need to be held at that angle when they're mitered or coped. This jig adjusts to hold different sized moldings.

FC82

CUTOFF BAR

This jig replaces your miter gauge for general crosscutting. It's more accurate because it rides in *both* miter gauge slots, and it features a chip shield for added safety.

TS43

CORNER ASSEMBLY JIG

Use this jig to glue delicate right-angle assemblies or ones that can't be clamped directly.

JF60

CUTOFF JIG

This sliding cutoff jig lets you crosscut long and wide boards more accurately than you can using just a miter gauge. It includes a sliding stop for convenient repetitive cuts, as well as an acrylic chip guard.

JW32

CORNER SQUARE

This little clamping aid takes the guesswork out of getting square corners when assembling cabinets and drawers.

GC70

CUTOFF TABLE, SLIDING

The fence on this sliding table has two mounting positions, forward and back, yielding angle adjustments with a range of of 115 degrees. The sliding stop stores on the back of the fence when not in use.

JF89; see also TS94

COVING FENCE

This adjustable-angle fence attaches directly to your table saw fence and locks securely at any angle, eliminating the need for clamps and a straightedge when cutting coves on the table saw.

TS89

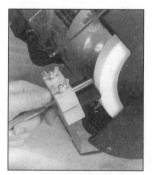

DIAMOND-POINT DRESSER HOLDER

A grinding wheel needs to be "dressed" routinely to shape the wheel and expose fresh abrasive. This clamp holds a diamond wheel dresser; slide the clamp against the tool rest for accurate dressing.

S38

KEY: AR—ADVANCED ROUTING; **BC**—MAKING BOXES AND CHESTS; **BIC**—MAKING BUILT-IN CABINETS; **BS**—USING THE BAND SAW; **DB**—MAKING DESKS AND BOOKCASES; **DP**—USING THE DRILL PRESS; **F**—FINISHING; **FC**—FINISH CARPENTRY; **GC**—GLUING AND CLAMPING; **HT**—USING HAND TOOLS; **JF**—MAKING JIGS AND FIXTURES;

DISC-AND-DRUM SANDER

Sand flat and convex shapes with the 10-inch disc on this sander, and concave surfaces with the drum. The sander requires a double-shaft motor.

SP108

DOVETAIL LAYOUT RULE

Lay out evenly spaced dovetails accurately with this layout rule. Just choose the number of tails and the space you want between them, and this jig will do the rest.

JW90

DISC SANDER COMPASS JIG

This jig will quickly true up *and* smooth a bandsawn circular part. It's made from two pieces of plywood—the base clamps to a sanding table, and the adjustable top has holes for a pivot pin.

SP69; see also JF35

DOVETAIL SLOPE GAUGE

This simple slope gauge saves you from setting a sliding bevel every time you cut dovetails. Make one for each of your favorite dovetail angles.

JW91

DOOR BUCK

The weight of the door flexes these door bucks, causing the jaws to pinch the door and hold it tight when trimming, routing mortises, or drilling for hardware.

FC37

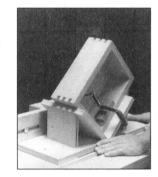

DOVETAIL SPLINE JIG

Decorative dovetail splines add strength and beauty to plain mitered box corners. This sliding carriage for your router table makes them easy to cut.

RS66

DOVETAIL CHISEL GUIDE

This guide ensures all your cross-grain chisel cuts are in a perfect line. It also holds the tail board in place over the pin board, just like a commercial dovetail jig.

JW91

DOVETAIL TABLE, BAND SAW

This auxiliary table pivots in either direction, ensuring uniform slope when cutting dovetail pins on the band saw.

BS88

JW—Joining Wood; **RS**—Routing and Shaping; **S**—Sharpening; **SP**—Sanding and Planing; **SS**—Using the Scroll Saw; **TC**—Making Tables and Chairs; **TS**—Using the Table Saw; **WSF**—Workbenches and Shop Furniture; **WWM**—Wood and Woodworking Materials

DOWEL MAKER

Make your own dowels with this router table jig. Push a length of square stock through the jig, using a drill to rotate the stock as it moves past a straight cutter.

AR69

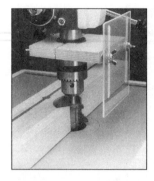

DRILL PRESS ROUTING GUARD

This guard clamps to the drill chuck and shields your hands when using router bits for shaping on the drill press.

DP86

DRILL GUIDE FOR DOWELED MITERS

This jig aids in drilling a hole through a mitered corner. Fill the hole with a dowel and, when sanded flush, the dowel appears oval—a unique decorative touch.

BC33

DRILL PRESS STAND

Here is an easy-to-build stand and economical cabinet for storing all your drill press accessories. It features simple case-and-drawer construction and rolls on heavy-duty 3-inch casters.

DP108

DRILL PRESS FOOT SWITCH

Use your foot to operate both the On/Off switch and the quill on a drill press. This device frees both hands for increased safety and accuracy.

DP40

DRILL PRESS STORAGE TRAY

Keep all your drill bits organized and close at hand with this storage tray. It mounts to the drill press and can be removed for bench use.

DP21

DRILL PRESS QUILL LOCK

A quill lock is essential when using the drill press for drum sanding, sharpening, or shaping. It prevents damage to the quill that can be caused by the sideways thrust these operations produce.

DP93

DRILL PRESS TABLE, TILTING

This drill press table has a sliding fence with adjustable flip stops, replaceable collars, sliding hold-downs, and a tilting mechanism for angled holes.

JF111; see also DP31

KEY: **AR**—Advanced Routing; **BC**—Making Boxes and Chests; **BIC**—Making Built-In Cabinets; **BS**—Using the Band Saw; **DB**—Making Desks and Bookcases; **DP**—Using the Drill Press; **F**—Finishing; **FC**—Finish Carpentry; **GC**—Gluing and Clamping; **HT**—Using Hand Tools; **JF**—Making Jigs and Fixtures;

DRILL PRESS TABLE, VERTICAL

With this table you can accurately drill into the end grain of a workpiece for doweling and mortising.

DP64

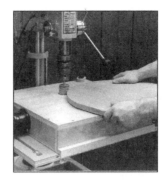

DRUM-SANDING TABLE

This table gives you a professional drum-sanding setup on your drill press, plus a built-in dust-collection port. Made from plywood, it has collar inserts for different size drums.

DP83; see also JF24

DRILL PRESS TILTING WORK SURFACE

This drill press table adjusts from 0 to 60 degrees in precise 15 degree increments using a set of tamboured wedges.

DP31; see also JF111

EGG CRATES

Egg crates let you organize your tools efficiently in perfectly fitting compartments. You can make them up in batches of different sizes and use them wherever a drawer needs organizing.

WSF73

DRILL PRESS TURNING JIG

Turn small parts like pulls, knobs, and finials on the drill press with this jig. The tool rest is adjustable on a plywood base. The drive center is made from a carriage bolt.

BC76; see also DP89

EXPANDER

This "clamp" works in reverse, spreading things apart, which is useful for assembling and disassembling chairs.

GC101; see also JF50

DRILL PRESS V-JIG

This V-shaped cradle holds cylinders for drilling on a drill press. A simple metal strap clamps a cylinder to the jig.

TC79; see also DP76

FEATHERBOARD, ADJUSTABLE

This featherboard slides in a slotted bar so you can easily position the featherboard anywhere on a machine table.

TS30

JW—Joining Wood; RS—Routing and Shaping; S—Sharpening; SP—Sanding and Planing; SS—Using the Scroll Saw; TC—Making Tables and Chairs; TS—Using the Table Saw; WSF—Workbenches and Shop Furniture; WWM—Wood and Woodworking Materials

FEATHERBOARD, HAND-HELD

When you can't clamp a featherboard to a machine, use this hand-held version to help guide the workpiece.

JF20

FENCE, AUXILIARY

This fence works like a T-square table saw fence, except that a movable jaw on the bottom lets you clamp the fence directly to a workpiece for routing and other cuts that require a fence.

JF65

FEATHERBOARD, JOINTER

Accurate edge jointing depends on keeping the stock tight to the fence. This featherboard is made from sturdy Baltic Birch plywood and gets bolted securely to the jointer.

SP20

FENCE STOPS, HINGED

The sliding stops on this fence are hinged to flip up out of the way so you can drill multiple holes in a piece of stock, even when the hole spacing is irregular.

DP79

FEATHERBOARD, UNIVERSAL

Use this jig with the Auxiliary Fence (this page) to eliminate the difficulty of clamping featherboards to a machine table. The featherboard slides anywhere along the fence and locks securely.

JF69

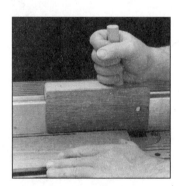

FENCE STRADDLER PUSH STICK

For very narrow rip cuts, this fence straddler acts as both a push stick and a hold-down.

TS55

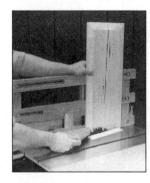

FENCE, ADJUSTABLE-HEIGHT

This fence adjusts from 6 to 12 inches high for sawing or shaping boards on edge. It's especially suitable for resawing, when you want the fence just slightly lower than the width of the board.

JF80

FINGER-JOINT JIG

Strong finger joints require that the fingers and the space between them be identical, and that's what this jig ensures. The sliding fence makes it easy to find the right spacing and keep it.

JW84; see also AR13, BC27

KEY: AR—Advanced Routing; **BC**—Making Boxes and Chests; **BIC**—Making Built-In Cabinets; **BS**—Using the Band Saw; **DB**—Making Desks and Bookcases; **DP**—Using the Drill Press; **F**—Finishing; **FC**—Finish Carpentry; **GC**—Gluing and Clamping; **HT**—Using Hand Tools; **JF**—Making Jigs and Fixtures;

FINISHING BOOTH, PORTABLE

Keep the dust off your just-finished projects with this portable finishing booth. It includes a fan that speeds drying. (Designed for brushed and rubbed-on finishes only, not for sprayed finishes.)

F79

FRAME CLAMP

Assemble perfectly mitered picture frames with this clamp. A single screw pulls all four corners evenly.

GC115

FLUSH-CUT SAW

This shop-made saw's teeth are set to one side only so you can flush-cut dowels, pegs, and wedges without scratching the surrounding wood. The broad handle puts control right under your hand.

HT105

FRET-SAWING TABLE

This little table clamps into a vise and supports a workpiece when you're making delicate cuts with either a coping saw or a fret saw.

HT31

FLUSH-TRIM ROUTER BASE

This scrapwood router base plate lets you trim glued-on edgings so they're perfectly flush with case parts or countertops, eliminating tedious hand planing and sanding.

RS51; see also BIC68

GO-BARS

These go-bars make it easy to clamp a broad surface, like a veneered panel, against a benchtop. The bars are tightened between the workpiece and a U-shaped frame that's clamped to the bench.

WSF42

FLUTING JIG

This jig indexes spindles on your lathe and locks them in place so you can rout mortises, flutes, reeds, and any other cut parallel to the length of the stock.

AR60

GRINDER, FLAT

This grinder does the same job as a motorized whetstone, only better. It accommodates interchangable tool rests, as well as a set of sharpening stones, for a complete sharpening system.

S86

GRINDER, HOLLOW

You can overcome the drawbacks of typical grinding wheels with this grinder. The two-grit wheel is extra wide and has a buffing head as well. A slow-speed motor keeps tools cool.

S95

HAND SCREW, TRADITIONAL

The 1-inch-diameter wooden threads on these clamps let you apply plenty of pressure, and they are less likely than metal clamps to mar your work.

GC93

GRINDER TOOL REST

This tool rest replaces the inadequate one that likely came with your grinder. It's a single piece of ⅜-inch plywood spanning both grinding wheels so you can keep the angle the same on coarse and fine wheels.

S34

HAND SCREW CLAMP RACK

Keep your hand screws accessible and organized on this wall-mounted rack with adjustable dividers.

GC31

GRINDING GUIDE BLOCKS

Without the proper bevel grind, skew chisels and carving tools won't cut. These plywood guide blocks clamp to the tool rest on a motorized whetstone and ensure a perfect grind.

S56

HEIGHT GAUGE

This precision gauge takes the guesswork out of height adjustments and works equally well when setting router bits, shaper cutters, saw blades, and dado heads.

RS29

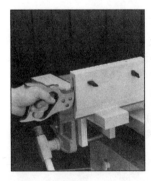

HANDSAW DEPTH STOP

Half-laps, dovetails, tenons, and other joints cut by hand will fit better if you saw with this jig, which stops the saw cut at a precise depth.

HT9

HEIGHT GAUGE WITH STAND

This gauge shows you the exact height of a saw blade or router bit because it references directly between the bit or blade and the table.

TS69

KEY: **AR**—Advanced Routing; **BC**—Making Boxes and Chests; **BIC**—Making Built-In Cabinets; **BS**—Using the Band Saw; **DB**—Making Desks and Bookcases; **DP**—Using the Drill Press; **F**—Finishing; **FC**—Finish Carpentry; **GC**—Gluing and Clamping; **HT**—Using Hand Tools; **JF**—Making Jigs and Fixtures;

HINGE-MORTISING TEMPLATE

This jig ensures that door hinges fit snugly in their mortises. It works on any size door and can be adjusted for different backsets.

FC37

HONING GUIDE FOR GOUGES

Honing the curved edge of a carving tool is easy with this adjustable guide. It moves forward and back like a chisel honing guide, while the tool holder swivels.

S56

HOLD-DOWN

Hold a workpiece securely anywhere on your benchtop with this device. It will fit into existing bench dog holes, or you can drill new holes as you need them.

GC109

INDEXING WHEEL FOR OVERARM ROUTER

Use this indexing wheel in conjunction with the Overhead Routing Jig (page 77) to rout any number of equally spaced flutes, grooves, or beads on a turned cylinder.

RS86

HOLE SPACING FIXTURE

Drill unlimited numbers of evenly spaced holes with this drill press fence attachment. The fixture clamps to a T-slot in the fence and adjusts for stock up to 2 inches thick.

DP56

JEWELER'S SAW TABLE

Cut delicate shapes for inlay, banding, marquetry, and parquetry with a jeweler's saw and this simple table.

AR79

HONING GUIDE

Holding a chisel or plane iron at the right angle is the key to good sharpening. This honing guide is made from a few scraps of wood and a few pieces of common hardware.

S28

JOINT-MAKING JIG

Mount a router *horizontally* in a table and you can better perform dozens of operations like mortising, tenoning, and cutting tongues or grooves because the stock rests flat on the table instead of on edge.

RS104

JW—JOINING WOOD; RS—ROUTING AND SHAPING; S—SHARPENING; SP—SANDING AND PLANING; SS—USING THE SCROLL SAW; TC—MAKING TABLES AND CHAIRS; TS—USING THE TABLE SAW; WSF—WORKBENCHES AND SHOP FURNITURE; WWM—WOOD AND WOODWORKING MATERIALS

JOINTER PUSH BLOCKS

Get safe, two-handed control over your face jointing with this push block, made from hardwood scraps.

SP20

L-BEVEL FOR SHARPENING

If you want to sharpen a tool to a specific bevel angle, this mini L-bevel will transfer the angle from a protractor to a honing guide.

S46

KNIFE HOLDER

Turn your drill press into an accurate grinder with this jig. It includes separate holders for sharpening jointer knives and chisels or plane irons.

DP92

LAMINATE-CUTTING GUIDE

Sheets of plastic laminate are unwieldy to handle and cut, even on a table saw. With this straightedge guide the laminate stays put, and the cut is made with a router and a ¼-inch straight bit.

BIC91; see also GC86

KNIFE-SHARPENING GUIDE

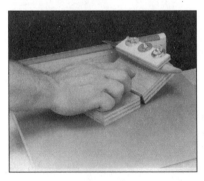

With this jig you can sharpen any short-bladed utility knife to a precise bevel.

S67

LATHE CHUCK

Make your own lathe chuck from a scrap of wood and a hose clamp. The chuck will hold small parts like turned box lids, finials, and drawer pulls.

BC16

KNOCK-DOWN CUTTING GRID

Two knock-down sawhorses connected by 8-foot 2 × 4s give you a huge, portable platform for cutting all kinds of sheet goods. It makes a great portable table as well.

JF121; see also WSF7

LATHE STEADYREST

A steadyrest prevents long and thin turnings from flexing under the pressure of a tool. This one clamps to the lathe bed and is adjustable for any size turning.

TC78

KEY: AR—Advanced Routing; BC—Making Boxes and Chests; BIC—Making Built-In Cabinets; BS—Using the Band Saw; DB—Making Desks and Bookcases; DP—Using the Drill Press; F—Finishing; FC—Finish Carpentry; GC—Gluing and Clamping; HT—Using Hand Tools; JF—Making Jigs and Fixtures;

LATHE TOOL REST FOR ROUTING

This fixture replaces your lathe tool rest and turns your router into a precision cutting tool for the lathe.

AR72

MITER CLAMP

Assemble perfect miters with this clamp that is made from a plywood base, a few blocks of hardwood, and readily available hardware.

GC104

LOG CARRIAGE

With this carriage and a band saw, you can turn a log into a pile of resawn lumber.

BS69

MITER GAUGE EXTENSION AND STOP

To make accurate crosscuts, you need to add a fence to any miter gauge. This one features a quick mount that attaches with wing nuts, and a sliding stop for repetitive cuts.

TS47; see also JF6

LOOSE TENON JIG

This jig holds the stock and guides a plunge router to cut matching "loose tenon" mortises in rails and stiles. A separate piece of stock serves as the tenon.

BC51

MITER JIG

This sliding miter jig has two adjustable fences so you can make right- and left-facing miters without having to switch a fence back and forth.

JW40

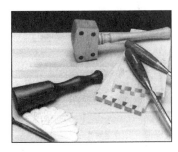

MALLETS, CARPENTER'S AND CARVER'S

Here are two sturdy, simple tools you'll use a lot. These mallets are designed for balance.

HT103

MORTISE-AND-TENON JIG

You can rout both mortises and tenons with this single jig. Both functions are done with a template guide, and the template itself is interchangeable for different size mortise-and-tenon joints.

AR9

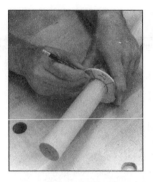

MORTISING COLLAR

This is a guide for drilling more than one hole around the circumference of a cylindrical workpiece, as where two stretchers join a chair leg.

TC74

MORTISING TEMPLATE, ROUTER

With this jig clamped to the workpiece and a template guide in your plunge router, you can easily rout mortises that are perfectly uniform.

AR4; see also JF27, JF36

MORTISING FENCE

Routing mortises on the router table requires a straight fence and stops that define the beginning and end of the cut. This fence combines both functions in a single jig.

JW67; see also JF42

NOTCH-SANDING JIG

This jig holds odd-shaped parts at a precise angle against a sanding belt or disc. It ensures that the angle is accurate and identical in multiple pieces.

SP69

MORTISING GUIDE, ROUTER

This is the simplest approach to guiding a plunge router when routing mortises. Two long supports clamped to the workpiece stabilize the router; the stretchers connecting the supports serve as stops.

AR3

OVAL TRAMMEL JIG

Rout circles *and* ellipses with this trammel jig. Attach the beam to a single fixed pivot for routing circles, or to a pair of sliding pivots for routing ellipses.

AR45

MORTISING JIG, ROUTER

Rout clean, deep mortises with this jig. It includes a sturdy table to clamp the work to, and an adjustable frame to guide the router.

RS64

OVERARM PIN HOLDER

Turn your router table into a pin router with this overarm pin holder. This jig includes plans for a Height Adjustor and Router Jack so you can make minute bit adjustments easily.

AR37

KEY: **AR**—Advanced Routing; **BC**—Making Boxes and Chests; **BIC**—Making Built-In Cabinets; **BS**—Using the Band Saw; **DB**—Making Desks and Bookcases; **DP**—Using the Drill Press; **F**—Finishing; **FC**—Finish Carpentry; **GC**—Gluing and Clamping; **HT**—Using Hand Tools; **JF**—Making Jigs and Fixtures;

OVERHEAD ROUTING JIG

Certain routing operations—like fluting or beading a cylinder—are best done with the router fixed *above* the work. This jig gives you overarm routing capability at minimal cost.

RS16; see also JF3

PATTERN-SAWING GUIDE

Similar to routing with a template, this jig lets you *saw* a workpiece to match a template using the table saw.

TS86; see also BIC46

PANEL CLAMP

These clamps are designed for assembling wide panels on edge. The double bars keep the joints flush, and a simple cam applies the pressure.

GC117

PIN-ROUTING JIG

This jig turns your router table into a pin router, which is especially useful for duplicating patterns on small workpieces.

BC10

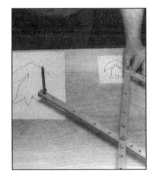

PANTOGRAPH

Enlarge or reduce shapes and patterns from photographs, drawings, and even real objects with this pantograph. It's made from thin hardwood scraps and common hardware.

SS60

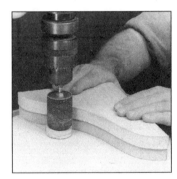

PIN-SANDING JIG

This jig lets you flush-trim a workpiece and smooth it at the same time. It consists of a plywood disc or "pin" mounted to a base.

SP69; see also DP84

PARALLEL RULE

With this parallel rule, you can find the correct fence angle for cutting coves on the table saw.

TS88

PIPE CLAMP

These pipe clamps were designed to sit flat on a workbench, and the laminated plywood jaws won't mar your work.

GC96

JW—Joining Wood; **RS**—Routing and Shaping; **S**—Sharpening; **SP**—Sanding and Planing; **SS**—Using the Scroll Saw; **TC**—Making Tables and Chairs; **TS**—Using the Table Saw; **WSF**—Workbenches and Shop Furniture; **WWM**—Wood and Woodworking Materials

PIPE CLAMP RACK

This clamping rack ensures your pipe clamps will apply pressure evenly along the same line when gluing boards edge to edge.

GC71; see also JF29

POCKET HOLE JIG

You can drill perfectly located pocket holes with this precision guide.

BIC64

PIPE CLAMP STORAGE BRACKETS

These wall brackets let you store your pipe and bar clamps horizontally, so they're less likely to fall.

GC32

POWER TOOL STAND, FOLDING

This stand supports any chop saw or benchtop machine for on-site work and folds flat when not in use.

FC95

PLANE-SQUARING JIG

Clamp this L-shaped block to your bench plane and you'll be able to plane board edges perfectly square to the faces.

HT42

PRESS BARS

These wooden bars, or *cauls*, are slightly crowned on one edge. When clamped against a wide surface, pressure is applied in the middle first and then outward toward the edges for even gluing pressure.

GC70

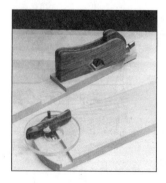

PLANES, SHOULDER AND ROUTER

These two specialty planes take care of all sorts of detailed trimming and fitting jobs on dadoes, rabbets, grooves, tenons, and more.

HT91

PROTRACTOR, MAGNETIC

This jig lets you accurately set the angle of chisels and plane blades in a honing guide in order to get a specific bevel angle.

S28

KEY: AR—Advanced Routing; **BC**—Making Boxes and Chests; **BIC**—Making Built-In Cabinets; **BS**—Using the Band Saw; **DB**—Making Desks and Bookcases; **DP**—Using the Drill Press; **F**—Finishing; **FC**—Finish Carpentry; **GC**—Gluing and Clamping; **HT**—Using Hand Tools; **JF**—Making Jigs and Fixtures;

PUSHER

This is an indispensable safety device, useful on the table saw, jointer, and router table. It combines a nose notch, rear notch, and a 45 degree V-notch, so you can safely push stock of all shapes and size.

JF63

RESAWING PIVOT FENCE

A single-point pivot resaw fence is the best type for general resawing. This one is simple to make from a few scraps and is easy to clamp in place.

BS63

PUSH STICK

This reversible push stick will ensure safe ripping of any size stock on the table saw, and it's especially well suited for very narrow stock.

TS29; see also JF19

RIP FENCE EXTENSION

This fence extension has a lip that helps support the weight of longer stock, making it ideal for cutting very long boards or pieces of plywood.

TS52

RAIL-AND-STRETCHER ROUTING JIG

Used with a router mounted horizontally, this jig cradles a chair rail or stretcher at the correct angle when mortising for "loose" tenon joints.

TC63

ROLLER STAND

Supporting long stock when cutting or shaping is crucial to safe woodworking. This adjustable roller stand features a wide wood roller and easy-to-adjust levelers so you can match the roller to your table height.

TS34; see also JF73

RESAWING FEATHERBOARDS

This jig has two featherboards that slide on a pair of dowels so you can apply side pressure to a workpiece at exactly the right height when resawing.

BS65

ROPE BRAKE

This jig lets you hold a workpiece securely to the benchtop without clamps. Instead, you apply pressure using a foot treadle attached to a rope that pulls down on a clamping bar.

WSF42

JW—Joining Wood; **RS**—Routing and Shaping; **S**—Sharpening; **SP**—Sanding and Planing; **SS**—Using the Scroll Saw; **TC**—Making Tables and Chairs; **TS**—Using the Table Saw; **WSF**—Workbenches and Shop Furniture; **WWM**—Wood and Woodworking Materials

ROUTER GUIDE, ADJUSTABLE

This jig makes cutting odd-size dadoes, rabbets, and grooves easier. It has a double fence system that can be adjusted for any width of cut greater than the bit you're using.

BIC61

ROUTER JOINTING FENCE

When you're jointing the edges of wide stock, this jig and your router table are good choices because the stock will lie flat on the table where it's completely supported.

RS54; see also SP16

ROUTER HEIGHT ADJUSTOR

This jig makes fine-tuning the bit height on a router table much easier. It attaches to any plunge router—even when it's not in a table—and makes height adjusting simple.

JF109

ROUTER MOUNTING PLATE

With this acrylic mounting plate, you can install your router from above a router table, giving you easy access for changing bits. The multiple inserts let you vary the bit opening for any size bit.

RS12

ROUTING JIG, MULTIPURPOSE

This jig doubles as both a small router table and an overhead routing jig.

JF4

ROUTER PLANING JIG

This jig turns your router into a thicknesser—it's ideal for precious pieces of figured wood that might chip out severely if fed through a planer.

RS52; see also SP34

ROUTER JOINERY POSITIONING JIG

This jig lets you easily and quickly make the precise fence adjustments needed for routing dovetails and finger joints or for making other repetitive cuts on a router table.

AR16

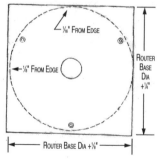

ROUTER SOLE FOR ODD-SIZE DADOES

Each edge of this base is progressively farther from the bit so you can widen dadoes by specific increments using a single, standard router bit. This is especially useful when working with plywood.

RS55

KEY: **AR**—Advanced Routing; **BC**—Making Boxes and Chests; **BIC**—Making Built-In Cabinets; **BS**—Using the Band Saw; **DB**—Making Desks and Bookcases; **DP**—Using the Drill Press; **F**—Finishing; **FC**—Finish Carpentry; **GC**—Gluing and Clamping; **HT**—Using Hand Tools; **JF**—Making Jigs and Fixtures;

ROUTER TABLE

This benchtop router table takes up little space and features a miter gauge slot, split fence, drop-in router mounting plate, and dust collection port.

RS97

ROUTER TABLE, LIFT-TOP

Changing bits is far easier on this router table, and you can do it without moving the fence (which has a built-in dust pickup). The bit guard doubles as a height gauge.

JF98

ROUTER WORKBENCH

In addition to being a standard router table, this routing station is designed to work with two other routing jigs—the Overhead Routing Jig (page 77) and the Mortise-and-Tenon Jig (page 75).

AR103

SANDING BLOCKS

These sanding blocks can be easily made from scrap wood. They have rubber or leather soles and beveled edges for getting into corners. The paper is held to the block with a rubber band set in a V-groove.

SP55

SANDPAPER DISPENSER

Designed to hold rolls of 4½-inch-wide sandpaper, this dispenser has a built-in measuring guide so you tear off exactly the length you need.

SP118

SAW-SHARPENING GUIDE BLOCKS

These blocks have a saw kerf cut at the correct angle for filing the teeth of a handsaw.

S75; see also HT35

SCRAPER PLANE

Combine the best features of a hand scraper and a bench plane in this wooden scraper plane. It uses a standard plane blade that's ground and burnished like a cabinet scraper blade.

SP88

SCRATCH STOCK

This scratch stock is especially useful on woods that would chip out if routed. The handle is turned for comfort, and the L-shape of the body provides a built-in fence.

HT50

JW—JOINING WOOD; RS—ROUTING AND SHAPING; S—SHARPENING; SP—SANDING AND PLANING; SS—USING THE SCROLL SAW; TC—MAKING TABLES AND CHAIRS; TS—USING THE TABLE SAW; WSF—WORKBENCHES AND SHOP FURNITURE; WWM—WOOD AND WOODWORKING MATERIALS

SCROLL SAW

This shop-made scroll saw is powered by a standard saber saw. It has a 20-inch throat, quick-release blade clamps, and a table that tilts 45 degrees right and left.

SS74

SCROLL SAW SAND BASE

This scroll saw base has a plywood box filled with sand. The dead weight reduces vibration, which in turn gives you smoother cuts.

SS26

SCROLL SAW BLADE-CHANGING FIXTURE

Make your own scroll saw blade-changing fixture from a few blocks of hardwood. Cutouts in the plate hold the clamps while you tighten the locking screws.

SS23

SCROLL SAW STORAGE STAND

This sturdy stand will hold your scroll saw and accessories. Patterns, manuals, and spare blades fit in the long, shallow drawers, and a bottom bin holds 150 pounds of sand to absorb vibration.

SS93

SCROLL SAW BLADE HOLDER

Keep scroll saw blades organized with this convenient storage rack. It's made from lengths of ½-inch PVC pipe and a block of wood.

SS17

SHAPER SLIDING TABLE JIG

Shape the ends of narrow stock safely with this sliding table jig. It has a sturdy hold-down clamp, an adjustable fence for angled stock, and a vertical table for cutting into the face of narrow stock.

RS47

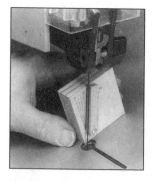

SCROLL SAW PROTRACTOR

Set your scroll saw table for angled cuts easily with this protractor. Just draw the angle lines from a pivot point on a small block of wood, and attach the indicator through the pivot point.

SS34

SHARPENING STATION

This cabinet is designed to support any sharpening machines you choose, as well as all the stones and accessories needed for a complete sharpening system.

S116

SHARPENING STROP

A strop loaded with a fine abrasive paste *polishes* an already sharp edge to an even finer degree of sharpness. The stropping surface is made from end-grain slices of hardwood to prevent the tool from digging in.

S31

SHAVE HORSE, BENCH-MOUNTED

This benchtop hold-down is modelled after the mechanism in a shave horse and it lets you hold stock securely using pressure from your foot or knee.

F46; see also JF53

SHELF PIN DRILLING GUIDE

A scrap of pegboard and two strips of wood are all you need to make this guide, which will ensure that shelf pin holes line up perfectly.

DB45

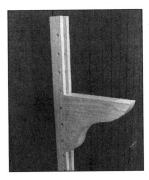

SHELF STANDARDS AND BRACKETS

An attractive alternative to the metal variety, these standards and brackets can be made with any wood to match your shelves. They're sturdy and won't scratch shelves as metal brackets do.

DB48

SHOOTING BOARD

This shooting board is basically a bench hook with a baseboard attached. With a workpiece held in the bench hook, you can "shoot" the end grain with the plane riding smoothly on the baseboard.

WSF47

SHOOTING BOARD/ MITER BOX

A shooting board lets you trim the ends of miters for a perfect fit. This jig combines a shooting board with a miter box and can be used to trim miters between 0 and 45 degrees.

FC73

SLIDING BEVEL

With this tool you can transfer angles accurately from workpiece to machine setups, and vice versa.

HT108

SPADE BIT SHARPENING JIG

This jig holds a spade bit securely, and it has angled bearing surfaces for filing the cutting edges of the bit. A thumbscrew raises the bit incrementally in the jig.

S81; see also DP45

SPINDLE-MARKING STRAIGHTEDGE

This L-shaped jig allows you to extend straight lines along the length of a cylinder, as when drilling for the stretchers that join chair legs.

TC74

SPLINED MITER JIG

This jig lets you safely cut slots for splined miters on the table saw. The jig cradles the rip fence for stability, and the clamp slides up and down for stock of different widths.

JW56; see also JF5

SPINDLE MORTISE DRILL GUIDE

This jig guides your drill when making mortises for chair spindles in both the seat and crest rail, so each spindle is angled and located accurately.

TC82

SPLIT ROUTING FENCE

This adjustable split fence for your router table lets you use your router as a mini shaper to joint stock and make full-edge profiling cuts.

RS30

SPINDLE STORY STICK

This jig lets you mark the locations for drilling into a cylinder so that the holes will be located identically in multiple workpieces.

TC75

SQUARE-CORNER SANDING JIG

This jig is designed to precisely sand square-cornered assemblies. The work is held against a miter gauge and pushed back and forth against a fence covered with sandpaper.

JF15

SPLINE MITER JIG FOR BOXES

You can strengthen and decorate mitered box corners by adding slips of contrasting wood. Cutting the kerfs for the slips is easy with this jig and your table saw.

BC30

STEPLADDER WORK TRAY

Reduce the number of trips up and down a ladder with this work tray. It locates the tools conveniently at waist height and makes it safer to work with tools on a ladder.

FC10

KEY: AR—Advanced Routing; **BC**—Making Boxes and Chests; **BIC**—Making Built-In Cabinets; **BS**—Using the Band Saw; **DB**—Making Desks and Bookcases; **DP**—Using the Drill Press; **F**—Finishing; **FC**—Finish Carpentry; **GC**—Gluing and Clamping; **HT**—Using Hand Tools; **JF**—Making Jigs and Fixtures;

STRIKING KNIFE

This striking knife features both an awl for marking with the grain and a bevel-edged knife for marking across the grain.

HT113

T-SQUARE ROUTER GUIDE

A T-square fence ensures your dadoes and rabbets will be perpendicular to the edge of the stock. This fence is quick to set up and accurate to use.

RS58; see also JF32

STRIP SANDER SHARPENING SYSTEM

This fixture turns a strip sander into a versatile sharpening system for chisels, gouges, and turning tools.

S107

TABLE SAW SLIDING TABLE

A multipurpose sliding table for the table saw, this jig includes attachments for tenoning, crosscutting, mitering, and holding odd-shaped pieces.

TS94; see also JF89

STRIP SANDER TOOL REST

Strip sanders make great tool sharpeners, but you'll need to replace the sander's table with a tool rest. This rest is made from a small piece of plywood and a length of angle iron.

S41

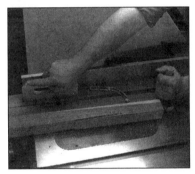

TAPERING JIG

Easy to make from a few small scraps of hardwood, this jig does the most consistent job of cutting tapered legs on the table saw.

TS82; see also JF6

SUPPORT STAND

This support stand has a hinged platform, so it functions as an extension table, too. The ball-bearing rollers allow movement in any direction.

JF73; see also TS34

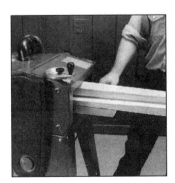

TAPERING JIG, PLANER

Use your planer to taper legs and other tapered workpieces with this wedge-shaped jig.

SP36

TAPERING JIG, VARIATION

This tapering jig grips the workpiece so your fingers don't have to, and it's wide enough to use comfortably without a push stick. It adjusts easily for any taper.

TC25; see also TS82, JF6

TENONING TEMPLATE JIG

This jig lets you rout the four sides of a tenon using a straight bit and a template guide. A fixed stop positions the work, and the broad template surface supports even a large plunge router.

AR6

TENONING JIG, ADVANCED

This tenoning jig features backstops that pivot between 90 and 45 degrees for cutting either straight or angled tenons.

JF84

THICKNESS SANDER

Unlike a planer, this 16-inch-wide thickness sander will handle thin stock and wood with difficult grain without chipout.

SP95

TENONING JIG, BASIC

This jig straddles the table saw fence and holds the workpiece perpendicular to the table for making the cheek cuts on a tenon. The fence adjusts for angled tenons as well.

JW73

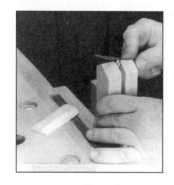

TWIST BIT SHARPENING JIG

This jig holds twist bits securely and ensures the cutting edges of the bit are filed at the correct angle. A thumbscrew raises the bit for precise honing.

DP44

TENONING JIG, ROUTER

This jig is designed for routing just one side of a tenon at a time. A big advantage is that you can clamp a whole project's worth of tenons together and rout them at one time.

AR5

VACUUM HOLD-DOWN

If you have a vacuum press, you can make this hold-down plate for holding flat workpieces securely without clamps.

JF55

KEY: **AR**—Advanced Routing; **BC**—Making Boxes and Chests; **BIC**—Making Built-In Cabinets; **BS**—Using the Band Saw; **DB**—Making Desks and Bookcases; **DP**—Using the Drill Press; **F**—Finishing; **FC**—Finish Carpentry; **GC**—Gluing and Clamping; **HT**—Using Hand Tools; **JF**—Making Jigs and Fixtures;

VENEER-CUTTING JIG

The best way to cut veneer is with a veneer saw or razor knife and this jig. The wooden bar serves as a clamp and straight-edge in one.

GC85

VISE MOUNT, TILTING

Tilting a bench vise gives you greater control over many hand operations like chiseling and carving. This hinged vise mount has a pivoting arm attached to one side to hold the work at the desired angle.

WSF36

VIOLIN CLAMP

This is a light-duty clamp, but it has many uses when you need pressure close to the edge of an assembly. It's made from plywood discs, a carriage bolt, and washers.

GC108

WEDGE, FITTED

For machines on casters, these wedges surround the casters and keep them from rolling or swivelling. They're especially suited to machines that vibrate.

WSF65

VISE JAW FACE, SWIVELING

This triangular block works with the Grooved Vise Jaw Faces (this page) and pivots to hold tapered workpieces.

WSF36

WEDGE, STEPPED

This wedge prevents a tool or cabinet on casters from rolling, and it has a flat surface at the top of the wedge that provides greater support than a plain wedge.

WSF65

VISE JAW FACES, GROOVED

These auxiliary jaw faces hold odd-shaped work securely. Vertical round-bottom grooves hold dowels, and a horizontal V-groove holds rectangular stock.

WSF34

WEDGE JACK

This device is made from a pair of wedges and a cam. Attached to a mobile tool or cabinet base, the jacks lift the cabinet off the casters by pressing down on the cam. The jack can be operated by hand or foot.

WSF65

JW—Joining Wood; **RS**—Routing and Shaping; **S**—Sharpening; **SP**—Sanding and Planing; **SS**—Using the Scroll Saw; **TC**—Making Tables and Chairs; **TS**—Using the Table Saw; **WSF**—Workbenches and Shop Furniture; **WWM**—Wood and Woodworking Materials

WHEELBARROW STAND

This is the easiest, least expensive, and most versatile approach to making a tool or cabinet mobile. It takes two casters instead of four and sits solidly on the ground until you need to move it.

WSF63

WORKSHOP SAWMILL

This device lets you take a rough log and cut it into a stack of boards. The log is always secured to the mill, which has a lip that rides against the table edge.

WWM52

REFERENCE
CHARTS

REFERENCE CHARTS

enable you to find a specific piece of vital information at a quick glance—the standard height of a dining table or chair, for example. They also provide direct comparisons of the tools and materials you work with—router bits, saw blades, finishes, and glues—so you can make the best choice for the job at hand. The 29 charts on the following pages form an up-to-date reference manual for dozens of these important woodworking choices.

TANGENTIAL AND RADIAL WOOD MOVEMENT

These percentages indicate how much you can expect a green board to shrink across the grain when it releases *all* of its bound water (from 28 percent moisture content to completely dry).

SPECIES	% TANGENTIAL MOVEMENT	% RADIAL MOVEMENT	SPECIES	% TANGENTIAL MOVEMENT	% RADIAL MOVEMENT
Domestic Hardwoods			**Domestic Softwoods**		
Alder, Red	7.3	4.4	Cedar, Aromatic Red	5.2	3.3
Ash, White	7.8	4.9	Cedar, Western Red	5.0	2.4
Aspen (Cottonwood)	6.7	3.5	Cedar, White	4.9	2.2
Basswood	9.3	6.6	Cypress	6.2	3.8
Beech	11.9	5.5	Fir, Douglas	7.3	4.5
Birch, White	8.6	6.3	Hemlock	7.9	4.3
Birch, Yellow	8.1	3.6	Larch	9.1	4.5
Butternut	6.4	3.4	Pine, Ponderosa	6.2	3.9
Catalpa	4.9	2.5	Pine, Sugar	5.6	2.9
Cherry	7.1	3.7	Pine, White	7.4	4.1
Chestnut	6.7	3.4	Pine, Yellow	6.1	2.1
Elm	9.5	4.2	Redwood	4.9	2.2
Hickory, Shagbark	10.5	7.0	Spruce, Sitka	7.5	4.3
Holly	9.9	4.8	**Imported Woods**		
Maple, Hard	9.9	4.8			
Maple, Soft	8.2	4.0	Bubinga	8.4	5.8
Oak, Red	8.9	4.2	Ebony	6.5	5.5
Oak, White	10.5	5.6	Lauan	8.0	3.8
Pecan	8.9	4.9	Mahogany, African	4.5	2.5
Poplar, Yellow	8.2	4.6	Mahogany, Genuine	4.1	3.0
Sweetgum	10.2	5.3	Primavera	5.2	3.1
Sycamore	8.4	5.0	Purpleheart	6.1	3.2
Walnut	7.8	5.5	Rosewood, Brazilian	4.6	2.9
Willow	8.7	3.3	Rosewood, Indian	5.8	2.7
			Teak	5.8	2.5

WOOD HAZARDS

While prolonged exposure to *all* types of sawdust can be unhealthy, certain species may cause physical problems after a short exposure. These are classified as *toxic* woods.

Reactions to toxic woods fall into two categories — *respiratory* and *skin and eye* ailments. Respiratory problems include bronchial disorders, asthma, rhinitis, and mucosal irritations. Skin and eye reactions include dermatitis, conjunctivitis, itching, and rashes.

TOXIC WOODS AND POTENTIAL HEALTH RISKS

SPECIES	RESPIRATORY AILMENTS	SKIN AND EYE IRRITATION
Arborvitae	X	
Ayan		X
Blackwood, African		X
Boxwood	X	X
Cashew		X
Cedar, Western Red	X	X
Cocobolo		X
Cocus		X
Dahoma	X	
Ebony	X	X
Greenheart	X	X
Guarea	X	
Iroko	X	X
Katon	X	
Lacewood	X	X
Lapacho	X	X
Mahogany, African	X	X
Mahogany, Honduras	X	X
Makore	X	X
Mansonia	X	X
Obeche	X	X
Opepe	X	X
Peroba Rosa	X	X
Peroba, White	X	X
Ramin		X
Redwood	X	
Rosewood, Brazilian		X
Rosewood, Indian		X
Satinwood		X
Sneezewood	X	
Stavewood	X	
Sucupira		X
Teak		X
Wenge	X	X

RELATIVE WOOD STRENGTHS

There are several important ways to measure wood strengths. When choosing a wood species, you should first decide what kind of strength you're looking for. Engineers measure the *compressive strength* (1) by loading a block of wood parallel to the grain until it breaks, and the *bending strength* (2) by loading a block perpendicular to the grain. Both are expressed in pounds per square inch (psi).

Stiffness (3) is determined by applying a load to a large beam until it deflects a specific amount. This is usually given in millions of pounds per square inch (Mpsi). To find the *hardness* (4), engineers measure the force needed to drive a metal ball halfway into a wooden surface. This force is recorded in pounds (lbs). In each case, the higher the number, the stronger the wood.

SPECIES	SPECIFIC GRAVITY	COMPRESSIVE STRENGTH (psi)	BENDING STRENGTH (psi)	STIFFNESS (Mpsi)	HARDNESS (lbs)
Domestic Hardwoods					
Alder, Red	.41	5,820	9,800	1.38	590
Ash, White	.60	7,410	15,000	1.74	1,320
Aspen (Cottonwood)	.38	4,250	8,400	1.18	350
Basswood	.37	4,730	8,700	1.46	410
Beech	.64	7,300	14,900	1.72	1,300
Birch, White	.55	5,690	12,300	1.59	910
Birch, Yellow	.62	8,170	16,600	2.01	1,260
Butternut	.38	5,110	8,100	1.18	490
Cherry	.50	7,110	12,300	1.49	950
Chestnut	.43	5,320	8,600	1.23	540
Elm	.50	5,520	11,800	1.34	830
Hickory	.72	9,210	20,200	2.16	N/A*
Maple, Hard	.63	7,830	15,800	1.83	1,450
Maple, Soft	.54	6,540	13,400	1.64	950
Oak, Red	.63	6,760	14,300	1.82	1,290
Oak, White	.68	7,440	15,200	1.78	1,360
Pecan	.66	7,850	13,700	1.73	1,820
Poplar, Yellow	.42	5,540	10,100	1.58	540
Sassafras	.46	4,760	9,000	1.12	N/A*
Sweetgum	.52	6,320	12,500	1.64	850
Sycamore	.49	5,380	10,000	1.42	770
Tupelo	.50	5,520	9,600	1.20	810
Walnut	.55	7,580	14,600	1.68	1,010
Willow	.39	4,100	7,800	1.01	N/A*

* *Not available — these woods have not been completely tested.*

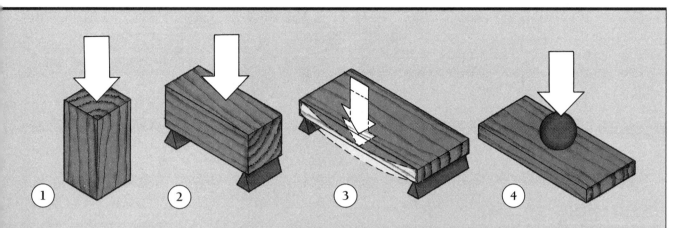

SPECIES	SPECIFIC GRAVITY	COMPRESSIVE STRENGTH (psi)	BENDING STRENGTH (psi)	STIFFNESS (Mpsi)	HARDNESS (lbs)
Domestic Softwoods					
Cedar, Aromatic Red	.47	6,020	8,800	.88	900
Cedar, Western Red	.32	4,560	7,500	1.11	350
Cedar, White	.32	3,960	6,500	.80	320
Cypress	.46	6,360	10,600	1.44	510
Fir, Douglas	.48	7,230	12,400	1.95	710
Hemlock	.45	7,200	11,300	1.63	540
Larch	.52	7,620	13,000	1.87	830
Pine, Ponderosa	.40	5,320	9,400	1.29	460
Pine, Sugar	.36	4,460	8,200	1.19	380
Pine, White	.35	4,800	8,600	1.24	380
Pine, Yellow	.59	8,470	14,500	1.98	870
Redwood	.35	5,220	7,900	1.10	420
Spruce, Sitka	.40	5,610	10,200	1.57	510
Imported Woods					
Bubinga	.71	10,500	22,600	2.48	2,690
Jelutong	.36	3,920	7,300	1.18	390
Lauan	.40	7,360	12,700	1.77	780
Mahogany, African	.42	6,460	10,700	1.40	830
Mahogany, Genuine	.45	6,780	11,500	1.50	800
Primavera	.40	5,600	9,500	1.04	660
Purpleheart	.67	10,320	19,200	2.27	1,860
Rosewood, Brazilian	.80	9,600	19,000	1.88	2,720
Rosewood, Indian	.75	9,220	16,900	1.78	3,170
Teak	.55	8,410	14,600	1.55	1,000

TRY THIS TRICK

Grind pieces of Arkansas and oilstone to any shape you want on a diamond bench stone. Use a coarse diamond stone to create the rough shape, then smooth the surfaces with finer grades.

SHARPENING STONES

TYPE OF STONE	ABRASIVE MATERIAL	BONDING AGENT OR PROCESS	AVAILABLE GRADES (U.S. GRIT)	COLORS
Arkansas Stones	Novaculite (quartz)	Geologic heat and compression	Washita (350) Soft Arkansas (500) Hard white (700) Hard black (900)	Multicolored Gray with green specks White Black
Synthetic Oilstones	Aluminum oxide (India) and silicon carbide (Crystolon)	Resin, sodium silicate	Coarse India (100) Coarse Crystolon (100) Medium Crystolon (180) Medium India (240) Fine India (280) Fine Crystolon (280)	Brown or tan Gray or black Gray or black Brown or tan Brown or tan Gray or black
Waterstones	Aluminum oxide or silicon carbide	Clay	250 Extra coarse (180) 800 Coarse (400) 1,000 Medium coarse (500) 1,200 Medium (600) 4,000 Fine (900) 6,000 Extra fine (1,000) 8,000 Ultrafine (1,200)	Tan, brown, or gray
Diamond stones	Diamond dust	Nickel (or another soft metal) fused to a steel plate	Coarse (240) Medium (320) Fine (600) Extra fine (1,200)	Silver gray; plastic bases are often color coded to help identify grades
Ceramic stones	Aluminum oxide	Ceramics, fused at 3,000°F	Medium (600) Fine (1,000) Ultrafine (1,200)	Gray White White

TRY THIS TRICK

Using spray adhesive, stick sheets of aluminum oxide or silicon-carbide sandpaper to finished hardwood blocks to create a versatile, low-cost sharpening system. Use 120-grit for coarse, 220 for medium, 320 for fine, and 600 for ultrafine. These abrasives need no lubricants, although you can use water with wet/dry silicon-carbide sandpaper. When the abrasive becomes worn or loaded, simply peel up the old sheet and stick down another.

CLEANER/ COOLANT	PREPARATION	CARE	SPECIAL CHARACTERISTICS
Light oil or water	Soak in cleaner/coolant prior to using first time	Wipe away dirty oil or water after each use; cover stone to keep from drying; scrub clean with oil or kerosene	Long wearing; produces an extremely keen edge; oil helps to protect tools
Light oil	None required	Wipe away dirty oil after each use; scrub clean with oil or kerosene	Extremely hard and long wearing; inexpensive; produces serviceable edge; oil helps to protect tools
Water	Soak coarse and medium stones in water prior to using	Rinse stones after each use; if stones are stored submerged, change water occasionally and keep from freezing	Many grades available; fast cutting; produces extremely keen edge; wears quickly; must be flattened more frequently than other stones; water may rust tools
None required	None required	Brush away filings; wipe occasionally with damp cloth	Extremely long wearing; stays flat; produces keen edge; can be used to sharpen carbide; very expensive
None required	None required	Wipe occasionally with damp cloth; scrub clean with soap and water	Extremely long wearing; stays flat; produces extremely keen edge; no coarse grits available; can be used to sharpen carbide; moderately expensive

MAXIMUM SHELVING SPANS (FOR 10-INCH-WIDE SHELVES SUPPORTING 20 POUNDS PER FOOT)

MATERIAL	MAXIMUM SPAN	MATERIAL	MAXIMUM SPAN
³/₄″ Particleboard	24″	³/₄″ Plywood, reinforced with a ³/₄″ x 1¹/₂″ oak strip glued edge to edge	33″
³/₄″ Plywood	30″		
³/₄″ Yellow pine	36″	³/₄″ Plywood, reinforced with two ³/₄″ x ³/₄″ oak strips glued to the bottom face	42″
1″ Yellow pine	48″		
1¹/₂″ Yellow pine	66″	³/₄″ Plywood, reinforced with a ³/₄″ x 1¹/₂″ oak strip glued face to edge	42″
³/₄″ Oak	48″		
1″ Oak	54″	³/₄″ Plywood, reinforced with two ³/₄″ x 1¹/₂″ oak strips glued face to edge	48″
1¹/₂″ Oak	78″		

STANDARD DESK DIMENSIONS

DESKS				
TYPE OF DESK	WORK SURFACE HEIGHT	OVERALL HEIGHT	OVERALL WIDTH	OVERALL DEPTH
Lap desk	4″–6″	4″–6″	20″–24″	12″–18″
Slant-front desk	28″–30″	40″–42″	36″–42″	18″–24″
Secretary	28″–30″	78″–84″	36″–42″	18″–24″
Writing table	28″–30″	28″–30″	36″–40″	20″–24″
Table desk	28″–30″	38″–68″	30″–48″	20″–30″
Pedestal desk	28″–30″	28″–30″	48″–72″	24″–30″
Rolltop desk	28″–30″	40″–48″	48″–72″	24″–30″
Typing table	24″–28″	24″–28″	36″–42″	16″–24″
Computer desk	24″–28″	24″–58″	24″–60″	20″–30″
Children's desk	20″–22″	20″–22″	24″–30″	18″–20″

DESK STORAGE				
COMPONENT	HEIGHT	WIDTH	DEPTH	LENGTH
Drawers*				
Above knee space	N/A	20″–24″	2″–4″	18″–28″
Beside knee space	N/A	12″–18″	4″–10″	18″–28″
Behind knee space	N/A	34″–40″	4″–10″	16″–22″
Letter file	N/A	12″†	10″	18″–28″
Legal file	N/A	15″†	10″	18″–28″
Compartments				
Envelope	4¹/₂″–7″	2″–3″	7″–10″	N/A
Stationery	1¹/₂″–2″	12″	7″–10″	N/A
Stamp drawer	1¹/₂″–3″	3¹/₂″–5″	7″–10″	N/A

*All drawer dimensions are inside measurements.
†For hanging files, add ¹/₂″ to the width and 1″ to the depth.

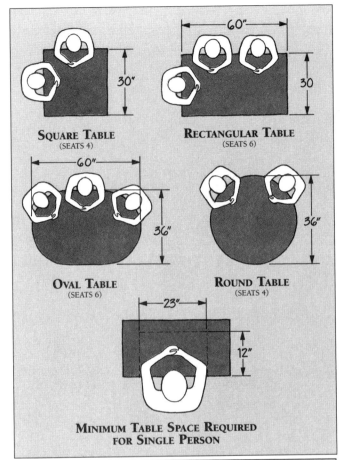

SQUARE TABLE
(SEATS 4)

RECTANGULAR TABLE
(SEATS 6)

OVAL TABLE
(SEATS 6)

ROUND TABLE
(SEATS 4)

**MINIMUM TABLE SPACE REQUIRED
FOR SINGLE PERSON**

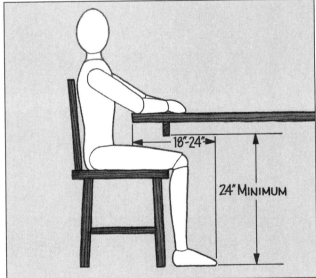

If you sit at a table, not only must there be enough room on top of it, there should also be adequate room underneath it. Leave at least 18 inches horizontally for toe room and no less than 24 inches vertically for your knees and thighs.

STANDARD TABLE DIMENSIONS

The dimensions shown for the following tables are averages. They are intended as guidelines, not absolutes. Use them as a jumping-off point in designing your own tables.

DINING TABLES

	NUMBER OF SEATS	HEIGHT	LENGTH	DEPTH OR WIDTH
Square	2	27"–30"	24"–26"	24"–26"
	4	27"–30"	30"–32"	30"–32"
	8	27"–30"	48"–50"	48"–50"
Rectangular	2	27"–30"	24"–26"	30"–32"
	6	27"–30"	30"–36"	66"–72"
	8	27"–30"	36"–42"	86"–96"
Round	2	27"–30"		24"–26" dia.
	3	27"–30"		30"–32" dia.
	4	27"–30"		36"–39" dia.
	5	27"–30"		42"–45" dia.
	6	27"–30"		48"–52" dia.
	7	27"–30"		54"–58" dia.
	8	27"–30"		62"–66" dia.
Oval	4	27"–30"	42"–48"	28"–32"
	6	27"–30"	60"–66"	32"–36"
	8	27"–30"	72"–78"	48"–52"

WORKTABLES

USE	HEIGHT	LENGTH	DEPTH
Food prep	34"–36"	30"–72"	23"–24"
Serving	36"–42"	42"–60"	15"–18"
Workbench	30"–40"	30"–72"	24"–30"

OCCASIONAL TABLES

USE	HEIGHT	LENGTH	DEPTH
Coffee table	15"–18"	30"–60"	22"–30"
End table	18"–24"	18"–24"	18"–24"
Hall table	34"–36"	36"–72"	16"–20"
Nightstand	24"–30"	18"–20"	18"–20"
Side table	18"–24"	24"–28"	18"–20"
Candlestand	24"–32"	15"–24"	15"–24"

SPECIALTY TABLES

USE	HEIGHT	LENGTH	DEPTH
Child's table	20"–22"	26"–30"	18"–22"
Computer table	25"–28"	36"–60"	22"–30"
Drafting table	32"–44"	31"–72"	23"–44"
Dressing table	29"–30"	40"–48"	18"–22"
Game table	29"–30"	30"–32"	30"–32"
Typing table	25"–28"	36"–42"	16"–24"
Writing table	28"–30"	36"–42"	20"–24"

Standard Cabinet Dimensions

Counter Unit
A. Depth . . . . 24″ to 25″
B. Height . . . . 36″
C. Width . . . . .12″ to 96″
D. Countertop thickness in kitchens
   and bathrooms . . . . 1¼″ to 1½″
   Elsewhere . . . . ¾″
E. Countertop overhang in kitchens and
   bathrooms .1½″ to 2″
   Elsewhere . . . . ¾″ to 2″
F. Backsplash height . . . . .4″ to 12″
G. Toespace depth . . . . 3″
H. Toespace height . . . . 4″

Wall Unit
I. Depth in kitchens . . . . .12″ to 13″
   Elsewhere . . . . 8″ to 15″
J. Height in kitchens . . . . 30″ to 42″
   Elsewhere . . . . Varies
K. Width . . . . .12″ to 96″
L. Height above counter . . . . .16″ to 18″

Tall Unit
M. Depth . . . . .12″ to 25″
N. Height . . . . .60″ to 84″
   (or to ceiling)
O. Width . . . . .12″ to 96″
P. Step-back or two-part design:
   Step or split occurs 36″ above floor

Corner Counter Unit
Q. Diagonal depth . . . . .43″ to 45″
R. Width . . . . 26″ to 38″

Corner Wall Unit
S. Diagonal depth . . . . 25″
T. Width . . . . 23″ to 24″

Doors
U. Height on base units . . . . .26″
   Elsewhere . . . . Varies
V. Width . . . . No more than 18″

Drawers
W. Height of top drawer . . . . 5″ to 6″
   Lower drawers become taller by 1″ increments
   up to 10″
X. Width . . . . Varies
   (often matches door above or below)

Shelves
Y. Depth of shelves . . . . To fit unit
Z. Depth of half-shelves in counter unit . . . 10″ to 12″
AA. Width . . . . Up to 36″
BB. Spacing . . . . 8″ to 16″

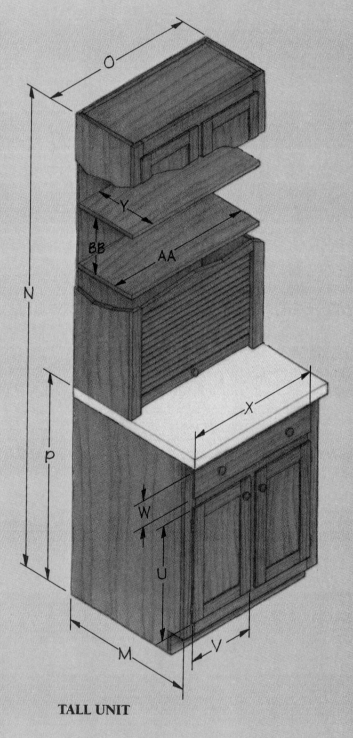

TALL UNIT

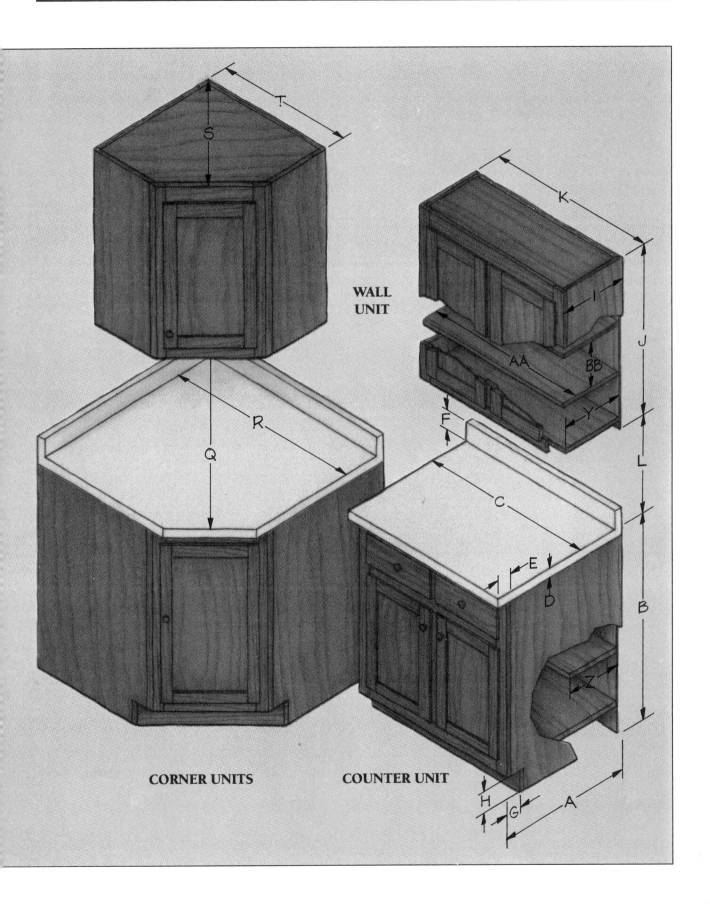

WALL
UNIT

CORNER UNITS   **COUNTER UNIT**

TRY THIS TRICK

To find the most comfortable configuration for a chair, make a mock-up from scraps of wood. Rest the seat on bricks or blocks of wood until you find a comfortable height and slope. Then add a back, leaning the boards against a wall.

STANDARD CHAIR DIMENSIONS

Like the chart "Standard Table Dimensions" on page 97, the following numbers are intended as guidelines to help design a usable chair. Designing a truly *comfortable* chair will require some experimentation to find the best possible configuration.

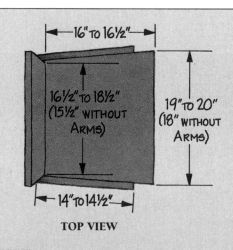

16" TO 16½"

16½" TO 18½"
(15½" WITHOUT ARMS)

19" TO 20"
(18" WITHOUT ARMS)

14" TO 14½"

TOP VIEW

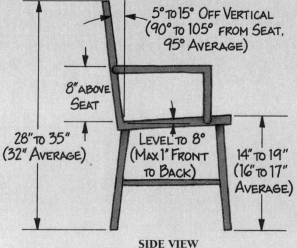

5° TO 15° OFF VERTICAL
(90° TO 105° FROM SEAT,
95° AVERAGE)

8" ABOVE SEAT

28" TO 35"
(32" AVERAGE)

LEVEL TO 8°
(MAX 1" FRONT TO BACK)

14" TO 19"
(16" TO 17" AVERAGE)

SIDE VIEW

DINING/DESK CHAIR

ADJUSTING FOR HEIGHT

The optimum (most comfortable) height for a table or chair changes with the height of the person using it. If you are building one or the other for a specific person, you may want to adjust the height of the chair seat or the tabletop accordingly.

Height of Person	Height of			
	Chair Seat	Dining Table	Typing Table	Worktable
60″	13.8″	24.5″	21.5″	32.4″
61″	14.1″	25.1″	22.1″	33.0″
62″	14.5″	25.8″	22.8″	33.7″
63″	14.9″	26.4″	23.4″	34.3″
64″	15.2″	27.0″	24.0″	34.9″
65″	15.6″	27.6″	24.6″	35.6″
66″	15.9″	28.3″	25.3″	36.2″
67″	16.3″	28.9″	25.9″	36.9″
68″	16.8″	29.5″	26.5″	37.5″
69″	17.1″	30.1″	27.1″	38.2″
70″	17.5″	30.8″	27.8″	38.8″
71″	17.7″	31.4″	28.4″	39.5″
72″	18.1″	32.0″	29.0″	40.1″

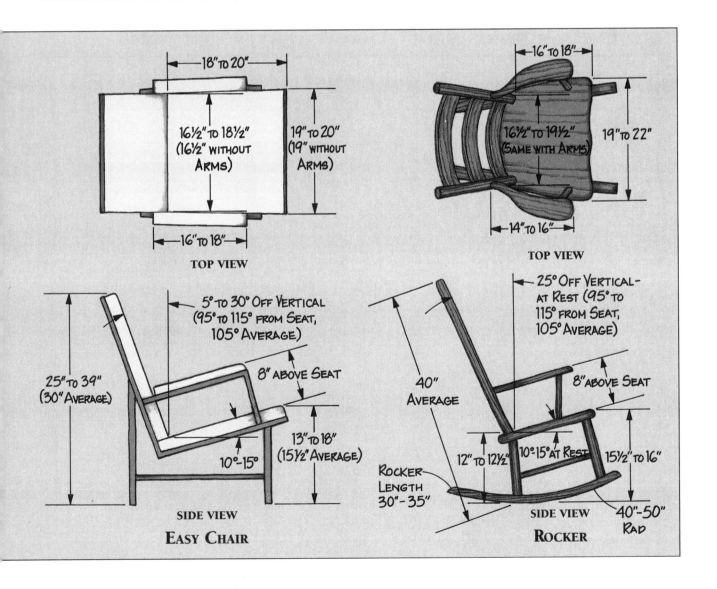

TOP VIEW

18″ TO 20″
16½″ TO 18½″ (16½″ WITHOUT ARMS)
19″ TO 20″ (19″ WITHOUT ARMS)
16″ TO 18″

TOP VIEW

16″ TO 18″
16½″ TO 19½″ (SAME WITH ARMS)
19″ TO 22″
14″ TO 16″

SIDE VIEW
EASY CHAIR

5° TO 30° OFF VERTICAL (95° TO 115° FROM SEAT, 105° AVERAGE)
8″ ABOVE SEAT
25″ TO 39″ (30″ AVERAGE)
13″ TO 18″ (15½″ AVERAGE)
10°–15°

SIDE VIEW
ROCKER

25° OFF VERTICAL AT REST (95° TO 115° FROM SEAT, 105° AVERAGE)
8″ ABOVE SEAT
40″ AVERAGE
12″ TO 12½″
10°–15° AT REST
15½″ TO 16″
ROCKER LENGTH 30″–35″
40″–50″ RAD

CHAIR WOODS

Have you ever owned a store-bought chair with joints that came apart no matter how you glued or reinforced them? Chances are, the errant chair parts were made from the *wrong wood species*.

Wood selection is more important for chairs than for any other woodworking projects. The joinery is subjected to the worst kinds of stress; many surfaces suffer continual abrasion. The wood must be able to stand up to this punishment; otherwise, the chair will come apart and no amount of glue can ever fix it.

There are several important rules of thumb for selecting chair woods. Most importantly, use hard wood for parts that must withstand heavy loads, such as legs, posts, rails, and stretchers. Use lighter, softer woods for extremely thick parts such as chair seats and armrests. This will cut down on the weight of the chair without affecting the soundness of the structure. However, never join softwood to softwood in a chair — the joint won't last.

If you need to scoop or carve a chair part, make it from a wood that can be easily sculpted. This same kind of common sense applies to chair parts that must be bent — choose a wood that bends easily.

WOOD SPECIES	FRAME MEMBERS	SEAT (SOLID)	SCULPTED PARTS	BENT PARTS	OTHER PROPERTIES
Ash	Good	Poor	Okay	Good	Light but very durable
Beech	Good	Poor	Poor	Okay	Splits easily if turning slender parts
Birch	Good	Poor	Poor	Good	Very hard to carve
Cherry	Good	Okay	Okay	Poor	Better suited for joined chairs
Hickory	Good	Poor	Poor	Good	Extremely hard and durable
Mahogany	Okay	Good	Good	Okay	Better suited for joined chairs
Maple	Good	Okay	Okay	Good	Best all-round chair wood
Oak, Red	Good	Poor	Poor	Good	Very strong grain, better suited for painted chairs
Oak, White	Good	Poor	Poor	Good	Best choice for bent parts
Pine	Poor	Good	Good	Poor	Typically used for seats only
Poplar	Poor	Good	Good	Poor	Typically used for seats only
Walnut	Good	Okay	Good	Poor	Better suited for joined chairs

WOOD BONDABILITY

WOOD SPECIES	SPECIFIC GRAVITY*	EXTRACTIVES†	BONDABILITY
Alder, red	.41	Medium	Good
Ash, white	.60	Low	Satisfactory
Basswood	.37	Low	Good
Beech	.64	Low	Poor
Birch	.60	Medium	Poor
Butternut	.38	Medium	Good
Cedar, aromatic	.37	High	Good
Cedar, western	.32	High	Excellent
Cherry, black	.50	Medium	Satisfactory
Chestnut	.43	Medium	Excellent
Cypress	.46	Low	Excellent
Ebony	.91	High	Poor
Elm	.50	Low	Good
Fir	.37	Medium	Excellent
Hemlock	.42	Medium	Good
Hickory	.72	Low	Poor
Larch	.52	Medium	Excellent
Mahogany	.45	High	Good
Maple, hard	.63	Low	Poor
Maple, soft	.48	Low	Satisfactory
Oak, red	.63	Medium	Satisfactory
Oak, white	.67	Low	Satisfactory
Pecan	.66	High	Satisfactory
Pine, white	.35	Medium	Good
Pine, yellow	.41	High	Good
Poplar, yellow	.42	Low	Excellent
Redwood	.35	High	Excellent
Rosewood	1.00	High	Poor
Spruce	.37	Medium	Excellent
Sycamore	.49	Medium	Satisfactory
Teak	.55	High	Poor
Tupelo	.50	Medium	Good
Walnut	.55	High	Satisfactory
Willow, black	.39	Low	Excellent

*When dried to 12 percent moisture content
†Relative concentrations

PROPERTIES OF COMMON ADHESIVES

TYPE	CLASSIFI-CATION	APPLICATIONS	GAP FILLING	SANDA-BILITY	COST
Cooked Hide Glue	Nonstructural/ Interior	General interior woodworking; antique restoration; veneering; joinery that can be easily disassembled	Fair	Good	Moderate
Liquid Hide Glue	Nonstructural/ Interior	General interior woodworking; complex assemblies requiring long open time; joinery that can be easily disassembled	Fair	Good	Economical
Polyvinyl Resin (White) Glue	Nonstructural/ Interior	General interior woodworking	Fair	Poor	Economical
Interior Aliphatic Resin (Yellow) Glue	Nonstructural/ Interior	General interior woodworking; gluing oily woods	Fair	Fair	Economical
Exterior Aliphatic Resin (Yellow) Glue	Semistructural/ Limited Exterior	General interior woodworking; gluing oily woods; kitchen and bathroom projects; outdoor furniture	Fair	Fair	Economical
Urea-Formaldehyde (Plastic Resin) Glue	Structural/ Limited Exterior	General woodworking; veneering; complex assemblies requiring long open time; architectural structures; bent laminations	Poor	Good	Moderate to expensive, depending on brand
Cyanoacrylate (Super) Glue	Nonstructural/ Interior	Small repairs; bonding nonporous materials to wood; securing inlays	Poor to fair, depending on formula	Fair	Expensive
Quick-Set Epoxy Cement	Semistructural/ Limited Exterior	Bathroom and kitchen projects; gluing oily woods; bonding nonporous materials to wood; repairs	Good	Good	Expensive
Slow-Set Epoxy Cement	Structural/ Exterior	Bathroom and kitchen projects; gluing oily woods; outdoor furniture; architectural structures; boat building; bonding nonporous materials to wood; securing inlays; bent laminations	Good	Good	Moderate to expensive, depending on quantity bought
Resorcinol Glue	Structural/ Exterior	Bathroom and kitchen projects; outdoor furniture; architectural structures; boat building; bent laminations; complex assemblies requiring long open time	Good	Good	Expensive
Mastics	Semistructural/ Limited Exterior	Securing plywood, wallboard, or foam to framing lumber, masonry, or concrete; non-load-bearing architectural structures	Excellent	Poor	Economical
Silicone Caulk	Nonstructural/ Interior	Bonding nonporous materials to wood	Good	Poor	Moderate
Contact Cement	Nonstructural/ Interior	Veneering; bonding plastic laminates to wood or wood products	Poor	Poor	Moderate to expensive, depending on quantity bought
Hot-Melt Glue	Nonstructural/ Interior	Simple projects; small repairs; temporary assemblies; joinery that can be easily disassembled	Excellent	Poor	Economical

WORKING TEMPERATURES (F)	CRITICAL TIMES				COMMENTS/CAUTIONS
	SHELF LIFE/ POT LIFE	OPEN ASSEMBLY TIME	CLOSED ASSEMBLY TIME	CURE TIME	
70°–100°, glue must be 125°–140°	Indefinite unmixed/ 1 day mixed	3–5 minutes	2 hours	12–16 hours	Develops tack almost immediately; nontoxic; don't heat glue above 160°F; clean up with water
70°–90°	1 year	15–30 minutes	12–16 hours	1 day	Low toxicity; clean up with water
60°–90°	Indefinite unopened, 1 year opened	5–10 minutes	1 hour	1 day	Nontoxic; freezing ruins uncured glue; clean up with water
45°–110°	18–24 months	5–10 minutes	30 minutes	1 day	Develops tack in about 1 minute; low toxicity; freezing ruins uncured glue; clean up with water
45°–110°	1 year	4–8 minutes	25–30 minutes	1 day	Critical times are slightly faster than interior formula; develops tack in about 1 minute; freezing ruins uncured glue; clean up with water
70°–100°	1 year unmixed/ 3–5 hours mixed	10–20 minutes	12–14 hours	1 day	Uncured glue is toxic to skin; cured glue dust (from sanding) is toxic when inhaled, so use adequate ventilation and protection; clean up with water
65°–180°	Varies with formula	15–30 seconds	1 minute	2–4 hours	Despite its interior classification, it is water-resistant; will bond skin, so use acetone to dissolve bonds; vapors can irritate nose and eyes and may cause headaches, so use with adequate ventilation
35°–200°, depending on formula	Indefinite unmixed/ 5 minutes mixed	1–5 minutes	5 minutes	12–24 hours	No clamping pressure required; uncured glue is toxic and may cause allergic reactions, so use adequate ventilation and protection; resists moisture and chemicals, but not heat — most formulas soften at 160°F; clean up with vinegar
35°–200°, depending on formula	Indefinite unmixed/ 1 hour mixed	30–60 minutes	2–4 hours	12–24 hours	No clamping pressure required; uncured glue is toxic and may cause allergic reactions, so use adequate ventilation and protection; resists moisture and chemicals, but not heat — most formulas soften at 160°F; clean up with vinegar
70°–110°	1 year unmixed/ 3 hours mixed	15–30 minutes	10–14 hours	1 day	Strongest of all glues; uncured glue is toxic to skin; cured glue dust (from sanding) is toxic when inhaled, so use adequate ventilation and protection; clean up with water
65°–110°	Indefinite unopened	5–10 minutes	2–4 hours	1 day	May irritate skin, nose, and eyes, so use adequate ventilation and protection; clean up with mineral spirits
65°–180°	Indefinite unopened	10–15 minutes	2–4 hours	1 day	Despite its interior classification, it is waterproof; may irritate skin, nose, and eyes, so use adequate ventilation and protection; clean up with mineral spirits
65°–180°	1 year	15–30 minutes	Bonds on contact	1 day	Vapors are highly toxic; solvent-based formulas are very flammable, so use adequate ventilation; clean up with acetone
32°–160°	Indefinite	5–10 seconds	30–60 seconds	1 minute	Glue may break down when exposed to some finishing chemicals; tip of glue gun is extremely hot, so be careful not to touch it

COMMON GLUING PROBLEMS AND SOLUTIONS

PROBLEM	POSSIBLE CAUSE	SOLUTION
Weak or failed joints	Not enough gluing surface	Redesign joint or add reinforcement to provide additional surface area.
	Not enough glue (starved joint)	Apply more glue. If gluing end grain, seal ends before gluing up.
	Wood moving in opposite directions	Align wood grain and annual rings so parts move in unison.
	Not enough pressure or uneven pressure	Apply more clamps. Space them evenly along joint.
	Glue line too thick	Apply more clamps. Make sure joint fits properly.
	Gaps and voids in glue line	Spread glue evenly over entire gluing surface. Make sure joint fits properly. If you want glue to fill voids, use epoxy cement or another adhesive with good gap-filling ability.
	Surface too rough	Plane, joint, or rout gluing surfaces if possible. Saw with smooth-cutting blade or sand to at least 50-grit.
	Wrong glue	Choose appropriate glue for particular wood species.
	Wood surface dirty or contaminated	Glue up joint as soon as possible after cutting it. If gluing surface is exposed for several days, lightly sand wood to clean it. If wood is oily, wipe with alcohol or naphtha.
	Shelf life or pot life expired	Purchase or mix fresh batch of glue.
	Assembly required too much time	Choose glue with longer open assembly time, or divide assembly into shorter steps.
	Glue not allowed to cure sufficiently	Leave assembly in clamps for longer period of time; wait for at least 24 hours before sanding or machining.
Creep or steps in joints	Wood moving in opposite directions	Align wood grain and annual rings so parts move in unison.
	Joints are too tight; pressure continues to squeeze hardened glue out of joints	Make sure joints fit properly.
Joints give slightly with time, but don't fail completely	Glue is creeping because of constant stress	Use a glue that is less likely to creep; redesign joinery to better withstand stress.
Sunken joints	Joints are machined or sanded before water from water-based glues can evaporate	Allow water to evaporate completely; wait at least 24 hours before sanding or machining.
Glue stains	Light stain — glue squeeze-out not properly cleaned from surface	If using water-based glue, scrape off excess and wash surface before glue dries. If using other glues, let dry completely, then scrape and sand. Check by wetting surface with water or naphtha.
	Dark stain — iron clamp in contact with joint as glue dried	Make sure pipes and cast-iron parts of clamps do not contact glue joint as glue dries.

PROPERTIES OF COMMON FINISHES

ENHANCING PROPERTIES

PENETRATION/DEPTH

Penetrating — Drying oils, rubbing oils, dyes, stains

Building — Shellacs, varnishes, polyurethanes, lacquers, waterborne resins, epoxies, oil and latex paints

> *Note: Drying oils and rubbing oils begin to build on the surface after the first or second coat. Most building finishes will penetrate on the first coat if they are thinned with the appropriate solvents.*

LUSTER

Flat — Most penetrating finishes after just one coat. Other finishes can be made to appear flat by adding flatteners or by rubbing them out with the proper abrasives.

Satin — Most penetrating finishes after several coats. Other finishes can take on a satin appearance by adding flatteners or rubbing them out with the proper abrasives.

Glossy — Shellacs, varnishes, polyurethanes, lacquers, waterborne resins, epoxies, oil and latex paints, provided there are no flatteners added. For high gloss, most finishes must be polished after curing.

> *Note: Wax adds gloss to a finish but has no luster of its own.*

TINT

Artificially tinted — Stains, dyes, oil and latex paints. Some varnishes, rubbing oils, and waxes are also tinted.

Natural amber tint — Rubbing oils, drying oils, shellacs, varnishes, polyurethanes, lacquers, epoxies, waxes

Clear (no discernible tint) — Waterborne resins; a very few lacquers, varnishes, and epoxies

OPACITY

Transparent — Rubbing oils, drying oils, shellacs, varnishes, polyurethanes, lacquers, waterborne resins, epoxies, dyes

Semi-transparent — Stains, thinned paints, transparent finishes with added flatteners or pigments, waxes

Opaque — Oil and latex paints

PROTECTING PROPERTIES

HARDNESS/ELASTICITY

Hard — Epoxies, polyurethanes, varnishes

Moderately hard — Lacquers, waterborne resins, oil and latex paints

Moderately elastic — Rubbing oils, shellacs (although shellacs become less elastic with time)

Elastic — Drying oils, stains, dyes, waxes

PERMEABILITY

Impermeable — Paraffin wax

Semi-permeable — Other waxes, shellacs, varnishes, polyurethanes, epoxies, oil paints

Permeable — Drying oils, rubbing oils, lacquers, waterborne resins, latex paints, stains, dyes

HEAT RESISTANCE

High heat resistance — Polyurethanes, epoxies, oils paints

Moderate heat resistance — Rubbing oils, lacquers, varnishes, waterborne resins, latex paints

Low heat resistance — Drying oils, shellacs

WATER RESISTANCE

Water-sensitive — Drying oils, some rubbing oils, shellacs, lacquers

Water-resistant — Some rubbing oils, waterborne resins, interior varnishes, polyurethanes, latex and oil paints

Waterproof — Exterior varnishes, polyurethanes, waterborne resins, latex and oil paints, epoxies

CHEMICAL RESISTANCE

Chemically sensitive — Drying oils, shellacs, waxes

Chemically resistant — Rubbing oils, lacquers, waterborne resins, latex paints

Highly chemically resistant — Varnishes, polyurethanes, epoxies, oil paints

DURABILITY

Highly durable — Varnishes, polyurethanes, epoxies, oil paints, dyes

Moderately durable — Shellac, lacquers, waterborne resins, latex paints, stains

Not very durable — Drying oils, rubbing oils, waxes

MISCELLANEOUS PROPERTIES

TOXICITY

Highly toxic — Epoxies, as well as some varnishes, paints, and rubbing oils

Moderately toxic — Lacquers, some varnishes, polyurethanes, some oil and latex paints, some stains, dyes

Moderately safe — Some drying oils, some rubbing oils, shellacs, some waterborne resins, some stains, some waxes

Nontoxic — Some drying and rubbing oils, some waterborne resins, some paints, some waxes

METHODS OF APPLICATION

Wipe-on — Drying oils, rubbing oils, stains, dyes, waxes

Pour-on — Epoxies

Brush-on — Shellacs, some lacquers, varnishes, polyurethanes, some waterborne resins, oil and latex paints

Spray-on — Some lacquers, some waterborne resins

> *Note: Not every specific finish will fit the neat pigeonholes in this chart. Depending on its ingredients, a particular brand of finish may display completely different properties from the norm. The information here should be taken as a general guide; there is not sufficient room to cover all the exceptions.*

HAZARDOUS FINISHING CHEMICALS (Ranked in Decreasing Order of Danger to Health)

NAME	CHEMICAL TYPE	USES	TOXICITY (TLV in PPM)*
EXTREMELY DANGEROUS			
1. Methylene Chloride	Chlorinated hydrocarbon	Paint strippers, furniture refinishers, paints	50
2. Glycol Ether†	Other	Lacquers, dyes, latex paints, spray paints, epoxies	5
3. Diglycidyl Ether†	Other	Epoxies	0.1
4. n-Hexane	Aliphatic hydrocarbon	Varnishes, rubbing oils	50
MODERATELY DANGEROUS			
5. Methanol	Alcohol	Paints, varnishes, lacquers, dyes, furniture refinishers, paint strippers	200
6. Acetone	Ketone	Paint strippers, wood fillers, lacquers, epoxies	750
7. Methyl-Ethyl Ketone	Ketone	Lacquers, wood fillers, spray paints	200
8. Petroleum Naphtha	Aliphatic hydrocarbon	Wood fillers, waxes, lacquers, general solvents	100
9. Toluol	Aromatic hydrocarbon	Polyurethanes, spray paints, rubbing oils, furniture refinishers, paint strippers, general solvents	100
10. Isopropanol	Alcohol	Wood fillers, lacquers	400
11. Methyl Isobutyl Ketone	Ketone	Wood fillers, spray paints	50
MILDLY DANGEROUS			
12. Xylene	Aromatic hydrocarbon	Lacquers, paint strippers, general solvents	100
13. VM&P Naphtha§	Aliphatic hydrocarbon	Lacquers, varnishes, general solvents	300
14. Turpentine	Other	Waxes, drying oils, rubbing oils, varnishes, general solvents	100
15. Mineral Spirits	Aliphatic hydrocarbon	Wood fillers, rubbing oils, varnishes, polyurethanes, stains, general solvents	200
16. Kerosene	Aliphatic hydrocarbon	General solvents	None
17. Ethanol	Alcohol	Shellacs, stains	1000

*Stands for "Threshold Limit Value in Parts Per Million."
†Stands for "Vapor Pressure in millimeters of Mercury."

VOLATILITY (VP in mm HG)†	DANGERS	SYMPTOMS OF OVEREXPOSURE
350	Affects skin, upper respiratory tract, blood, central nervous system, liver	Irritation, narcosis, numbness, heart palpitations, headache, shortness of breath, angina, heart attack
6	Affects skin, eyes, upper respiratory tract, central nervous system, kidneys, liver, reproductive system, blood	Headache, irritation, narcosis, kidney damage, pulmonary edema, fatigue, anemia
0.09	Affects skin, eyes, central nervous system, reproductive system	Irritation, allergies
124	Affects skin, upper respiratory tract, entire nervous system	Irritation, numbness, weakness, headache, nausea, loss of balance, weight loss, fatigue
97	Affects eyes, skin, central nervous system	Vision problems, optic nerve damage, blindness, narcosis
266	Affects skin, upper respiratory tract, central nervous system, eyes	Irritation, narcosis, dermatitis
70	Affects skin, upper respiratory tract, central nervous system	Irritation, narcosis, dermatitis
40	Affects eyes, skin, upper respiratory tract, lungs, central nervous system	Irritation, narcosis, dermatitis
22	Affects central nervous system, liver, upper respiratory tract, kidneys, skin, eyes	Irritation, dermatitis, narcosis, weakness, liver and kidney damage
33	Affects skin, upper respiratory tract, central nervous system	Irritation, headache, drowsiness
15	Affects skin, upper respiratory tract, central nervous system	Irritation, narcosis, dermatitis
9	Affects skin, upper respiratory tract, central nervous system, liver, gastrointestinal system, blood	Irritation, narcosis, dermatitis, stomach pain, incoordination, staggering
2–20	Affects skin, central nervous system, lungs	Irritation, dermatitis, narcosis
5	Affects skin, eyes, upper respiratory tract, lungs, central nervous system, kidneys, bladder	Irritation, dermatitis, pulmonary edema, narcosis, convulsions, kidney and bladder damage, fever
0.8	Affects skin, central nervous system, lungs, eyes	Irritation, dermatitis, narcosis
Varies	Affects skin, upper respiratory tract, lungs, central nervous system	Irritation, narcosis, lung hemorrhage, chemical pneumonia
43	Affects eyes, nose, skin, central nervous system	Irritation, headache, drowsiness, fatigue

†Although the volatility of these substances is low, they can be absorbed quickly through the skin. Even rubber gloves provide little protection.

§Stands for "Varnish Makers and Painters." This is petroleum naphtha with the more harmful hydrocarbons removed.

COMMON FLOOR FINISHES

TYPE	APPLICATION	COMMENTS
Polyurethane	Brush or roll on. Sand between coats.	Very durable but discolors in sunshine. Purchase a brand with a UV-inhibitor for sunny rooms. Relatively easy to apply and repair.
Water-borne finishes	Roll on. Finish is milky but dries clear. Sand between coats.	Fairly durable. Somewhat safer than solvent-based finishes. Very easy to apply and repair.
Oil finishes	Wipe on. Requires multiple coats. No need to sand between coats.	Not very durable. Won't protect against spills or abrasion. Extremely easy to apply and repair.
Acid-curing finishes	Add hardener, then brush or roll on. Sand between coats.	Extremely durable but highly toxic before they cure. Somewhat difficult to apply and repair. Also expensive.
Varnish	Brush on. Sand between coats.	Moderately durable. Fairly easy to apply and repair.
Shellac	Brush on. Sand between coats. Must be waxed or will spot.	Not very durable. Will not protect against spills. Produces very deep, warm finish. Easy to apply and repair.

ABRASIVE TYPES, GRADES, AND APPLICATIONS

TYPES		
MATERIAL	**COLOR**	**USES**
Flint	Off-white or tan	Removing wax, paint, and other finishing materials
Garnet	Pink or red-brown	Hand sanding
Aluminum Oxide	Tan or brown	Machine sanding
Silicon Carbide	Charcoal (wet/dry) or gray (dry only)	Sanding finishes

GRADES			
NAME	**GRIT NUMBERS**	**SYMBOLS**	**USES**
Extra Coarse	12, 16, 20	4½, 4, 3½	Grinding wood to shape
Very Coarse	24, 30, 36	3, 2½, 2	Grinding wood to shape, rough surfacing
Coarse	40, 50	1½, 1	Leveling surfaces removing stock, final surfacing
Medium	60, 80, 100	½, 1/0, 2/0	Smoothing surfaces, sanding joints flush
Fine	120, 150, 180	3/0, 4/0, 5/0	Preparing surfaces for "building" finishes such as varnish and polyurethane
Very Fine	220, 240, 280	6/0, 7/0, 8/0	Preparing surfaces or penetrating finishes such as tung oil and Danish oil
Extra Fine	320, 360, 400	9/0, (none), 10/0	Sanding finishes between coats
Ultra Fine	500, 600, 1,000	(none)	Sanding final finish

COMPOUND MITER ANGLES

FOUR SIDES			SIX SIDES		
SLOPE* OF FRAME	MITER GAUGE OR SAW ARM ANGLE†	SAW BLADE ANGLE	SLOPE* OF FRAME	MITER GAUGE OR SAW ARM ANGLE†	SAW BLADE ANGLE
85°	86°	44³/₄°	85°	87¹/₂°	29³/₄°
80°	82¹/₄°	44¹/₄°	80°	84³/₄°	29¹/₂°
75°	78¹/₄°	43¹/₂°	75°	82¹/₄°	29°
70°	74¹/₂°	42¹/₄°	70°	79³/₄°	28¹/₄°
65°	71°	40³/₄°	65°	77¹/₄°	27¹/₄°
60°	67¹/₂°	39°	60°	75°	26°
55°	64¹/₄°	36³/₄°	55°	72³/₄°	24¹/₂°
50°	61°	34¹/₂°	50°	70³/₄°	23°
45°	58¹/₄°	31³/₄°	45°	68³/₄°	21¹/₄°
40°	55¹/₂°	29°	40°	67°	19¹/₄°
35°	53¹/₄°	25³/₄°	35°	65¹/₂°	17¹/₄°
30°	51°	22¹/₂°	30°	64°	15°
25°	49¹/₄°	19°	25°	62³/₄°	12³/₄°
20°	47³/₄°	15¹/₂°	20°	61³/₄°	10¹/₄°
15°	46¹/₂°	11³/₄°	15°	61°	7³/₄°
10°	45³/₄°	7³/₄°	10°	60¹/₂°	5¹/₄°
5°	45¹/₄°	4°	5°	60°	2¹/₂°

EIGHT SIDES					
85°	88°	22¹/₂°	35°	71¹/₂°	13°
80°	86°	22¹/₄°	30°	70¹/₂°	11¹/₄°
75°	84¹/₄°	21³/₄°	25°	69¹/₂°	9¹/₂°
70°	82¹/₄°	21¹/₄°	20°	68³/₄°	7³/₄°
65°	80¹/₂°	20¹/₂°	15°	68¹/₄°	5³/₄°
60°	78³/₄°	19¹/₂°	10°	67³/₄°	4°
55°	77°	18¹/₂°	5°	67¹/₂°	2°
50°	75¹/₂°	17¹/₄°			
45°	74°	16°			
40°	72³/₄°	14¹/₂°			

*The slope of the stock's face, as measured from horizontal.
†For the proper saw arm setting, subtract the angle shown on the chart from 90°.

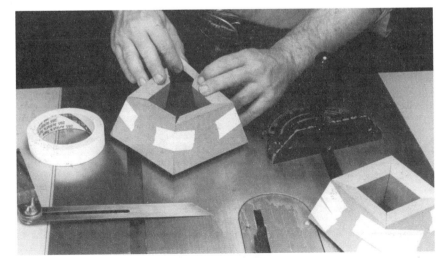

To check the setup, cut a test frame and assemble the members with masking tape. Measure the slope with a sliding T-bevel and a protractor. If the slope is *steeper* than you want, *decrease* the angle of the miter gauge. If it's *shallower, increase* the angle. Also inspect the joints. If they open on the *outside, increase* the tilt of the blade. If they open on the *inside, decrease* the tilt. Make these adjustments slowly, changing the miter gauge angle and the blade tilt no more than ¹/₂ degree at a time. You may have to cut several test frames before the setup is adjusted properly.

TWIST BIT SIZES

NUMBERED BITS							
Number	Decimal Equivalent	Number	Decimal Equivalent	Number	Decimal Equivalent	Number	Decimal Equivalent
80	.014″	60	.040″	40	.098″	20	.161″
79	.015″	59	.041″	39	.100″	19	.166″
78	.016″	58	.042″	38	.102″	18	.170″
77	.018″	57	.043″	37	.104″	17	.173″
76	.020″	56	.047″	36	.106″	16	.177″
75	.021″	55	.052″	35	.110″	15	.180″
74	.023″	54	.055″	34	.111″	14	.182″
73	.024″	53	.060″	33	.113″	13	.185″
72	.025″	52	.064″	32	.116″	12	.189″
71	.026″	51	.067″	31	.120″	11	.191″
70	.028″	50	.070″	30	.129″	10	.194″
69	.029″	49	.073″	29	.136″	9	.196″
68	.031″	48	.076″	28	.141″	8	.199″
67	.032″	47	.079″	27	.144″	7	.201″
66	.033″	46	.081″	26	.147″	6	.204″
65	.035″	45	.082″	25	.150″	5	.206″
64	.036″	44	.086″	24	.152″	4	.209″
63	.037″	43	.089″	23	.154″	3	.213″
62	.038″	42	.094″	22	.157″	2	.221″
61	.039″	41	.096″	21	.159″	1	.228″

FRACTIONAL BITS				LETTERED BITS			
Fraction	Decimal Equivalent	Fraction	Decimal Equivalent	Letter	Decimal Equivalent	Letter	Decimal Equivalent
1/64	.016″	17/64	.266″	A	.234″	N	.302″
1/32	.031″	9/32	.281″	B	.238″	O	.316″
3/64	.047″	19/64	.297″	C	.242″	P	.323″
1/16	.062″	5/16	.313″	D	.246″	Q	.332″
5/64	.078″	21/64	.328″	E	.250″	R	.339″
3/32	.094″	11/32	.344″	F	.257″	S	.348″
7/64	.109″	23/64	.359″	G	.261″	T	.358″
1/8	.125″	3/8	.375″	H	.266″	U	.368″
9/64	.141″	25/64	.391″	I	.272″	V	.377″
5/32	.156″	13/32	.406″	J	.277″	W	.386″
11/64	.172″	27/64	.422″	K	.281″	X	.397″
3/16	.188″	7/16	.438″	L	.290″	Y	.404″
13/64	.203″	29/64	.453″	M	.295″	Z	.413″
7/32	.219″	15/32	.469″				
15/64	.234″	31/64	.484″				
1/4	.250″	1/2	.500″				

RECOMMENDED DRILL PRESS SPEEDS (IN RPM) FOR DRILL PRESSES WITH HAND-OPERATED QUILL FEEDS

This chart lists recommended speeds for drill presses with *hand-operated quill feeds*. They are lower than maximum cutting speeds because most craftsmen tend to feed the quill much more slowly than industrial presses with power feeds. To get a smoother cut and prevent the bit from overheating, the speeds have been reduced to compensate for a slow feed. Use these speeds as a starting point. Drill several test holes, then adjust the speeds up or down to compensate for your own drilling technique.

MATERIAL	DIAMETER	TWIST	BRAD-POINT	SPADE	BORING	FORSTNER	MULTI-SPUR
Softwoods	1/8"	4,800	3,600				
	1/4"	2,400	3,600	2,400		2,400	
	1/2"	1,200	2,400	2,400	2,400	2,400	1,200
	3/4"	1,200	1,800	1,800	2,400	1,800	1,200
	1"		1,200	1,800	1,800	1,200	1,200
	1 1/2"			1,200	1,200	900	1,200
	2"					600	900
	3"					300	600
Hardwoods	1/8"	2,400	3,600				
	1/4"	1,800	2,400	1,800		1,800	
	1/2"	1,200	1,800	1,800	1,800	1,800	1,200
	3/4"	700	1,200	1,200	1,800	1,200	1,200
	1"		900	1,200	1,200	900	1,200
	1 1/2"			900	900	600	900
	2"					300	600
	3"						300
Ferrous Metals	1/8"	900					
	1/4"	600					
	1/2"	300					
	3/4"	150					
	1"	100					
Nonferrous Metals	1/8"	2,400					
	1/4"	1,800					
	1/2"	1,200					
	3/4"	600					
	1"	300					
Plastics	1/8"	3,600	3,600				
	1/4"	2,400	2,400			1,200	
	1/2"	1,200	1,800			900	900
	3/4"	600	1,200			600	600
	1"		600			300	300
	1 1/2"						150
	2"						100

COMMON BAND SAW BLADES

BLADE WIDTH	MINIMUM RADIUS*	GRIND	TEETH PER INCH†	USES AND COMMENTS
1/16"	0"	Standard	24	Fine scrollwork. Blade can turn a 90° corner because the kerf is as wide as the blade.
1/8"	3/16"	Standard	14	Cutting scrollwork that requires a smooth surface; also good for joinery
1/8"	3/16"	Skip	8	Fast cutting of scrollwork; cutting scrollwork in thick stock
3/16"	3/8"	Standard	10	Cutting small curves that require a smooth surface; joinery
3/16"	3/8"	Skip	4	Fast cutting of small curves; cutting small curves in thick stock
1/4"	5/8"	Standard	10,14,18	Cutting medium curves that require a smooth surface; joinery. Finer TPIs are best for joinery.
1/4"	5/8"	Skip	4,6	Fast cutting of medium curves in thick stock. For a good general-purpose blade, use 6 TPI.
1/4"	5/8"	Hook	4,6	Aggressive cutting of medium curves; ripping; resawing narrow stock
3/8"	1 1/4"	Standard	8,10,14	Cutting large curves which require a smooth surface; crosscutting and mitering thin stock
3/8"	1 1/4"	Skip	4	Fast cutting of large curves; crosscutting and mitering thick stock. This is also a good general-purpose blade for large saws.
3/8"	1 1/4"	Hook	4,6	Aggressive cutting of large curves; ripping; resawing narrow stock
1/2"	3"	Standard	6,14,18	Cutting gentle curves; crosscutting and mitering. Finer pitches will make very smooth, straight cuts.
1/2"	3"	Skip	4	Fast cutting of gentle curves
1/2"	3"	Hook	4,6	Aggressive cutting of gentle curves; ripping; resawing medium-size stock, sawing green wood. With green wood, 4 TPI works better.
3/4"	5"	Standard	6,8	Crosscutting and mitering thick stock
3/4"	5"	Skip	3,4	Fast cut-off work. May also be used to resaw softwoods.
3/4"	5"	Hook	3,4,6	Aggressive cut-offs; ripping; resawing wide boards; cutting green wood. With green wood, 3 TPI works best.
1"	8"	Standard	8,14	Continuous crosscutting; mitering of thick stock
1"	8"	Hook	3	Continuous ripping, resawing wide boards; cutting green wood

*Sources vary widely on the minimum radius that can be cut with any given band saw blade, and for good reason. The minimum radius depends not only on the width of the blade but also the set and kerf. These can vary from manufacturer to manufacturer. Consider the measurements in this column as estimates only.
†These are the pitches that are commonly available through mail-order suppliers. Other pitches may be available on special order.

COMMON TABLE SAW BLADES

TYPE	HOOK AND SPACING	GRIND	USES
RIP	20–25°, wide gullets High-Speed Steel Carbide-Tipped	Flat	Cutting parallel to the wood grain; ripping to width
CROSSCUT OR CUT-OFF	5–10°, narrow gullets High-Speed Steel Carbide-Tipped	Alternate top bevel	Cutting across the wood grain; cutting to length
COMBINATION	5–25°, narrow gullets alternating with wide gullets High-Speed Steel Carbide-Tipped	Alternate top bevel and flat	Ripping and crosscutting most woods and wood products
PLYWOOD	5–10°, narrow gullets High-Speed Steel Carbide-Tipped	Steep alternate top bevel (steel) or triple chip (carbide)	Cutting plywood; with carbide teeth will also cut composites
HOLLOW-GROUND PLANER	5–25°, narrow gullets alternating with wide gullets High-Speed Steel Only	Alternate top bevel and flat	Joinery; moldings; any operation requiring a smooth cut
THIN-KERF (Crosscut blade shown)	Depends on type; can be configured for rip, crosscut, or combination Rip Crosscut Combination Carbide-Tipped Only	Depends on type	Ripping or crosscutting hardwood

Common Molding Knives

SINGLE-PURPOSE KNIVES

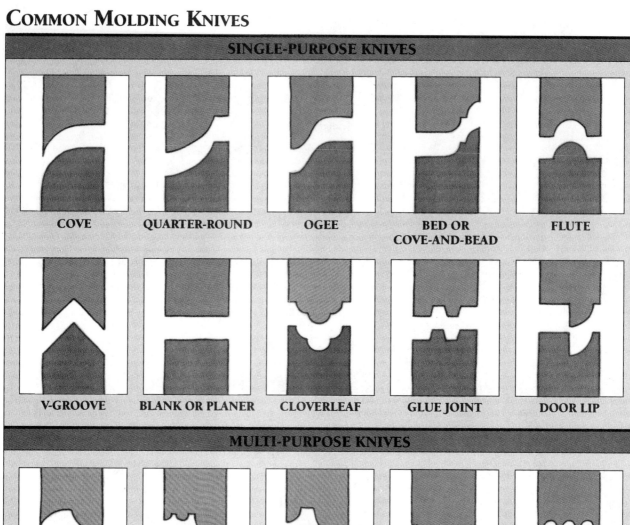

COVE · QUARTER-ROUND · OGEE · BED OR COVE-AND-BEAD · FLUTE

V-GROOVE · BLANK OR PLANER · CLOVERLEAF · GLUE JOINT · DOOR LIP

MULTI-PURPOSE KNIVES

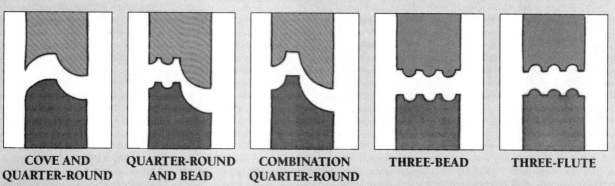

COVE AND QUARTER-ROUND · QUARTER-ROUND AND BEAD · COMBINATION QUARTER-ROUND · THREE-BEAD · THREE-FLUTE

COPING KNIVES

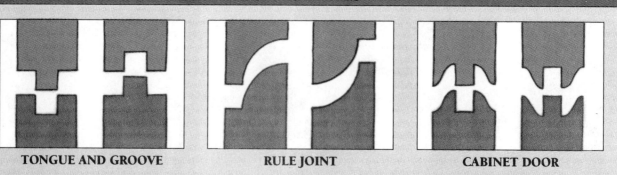

TONGUE AND GROOVE · RULE JOINT · CABINET DOOR

COPED JOINTS

REVERSIBLE JOINTS	FITTED JOINTS

DRAWER LOCK JOINT

To assemble the sides of lipped drawers to the drawer front.

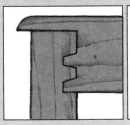 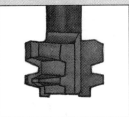

TONGUE-AND-GROOVE JOINT

To assemble boards edge to edge. Used most often in flooring and siding, but can also be used to glue up wide boards.

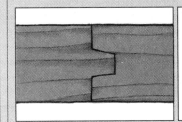 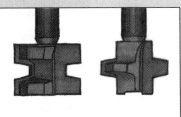

GLUE JOINT

To assemble boards edge to edge.

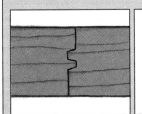 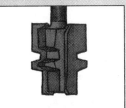

RULE JOINT

To make folding joints in drop-leaf tables.

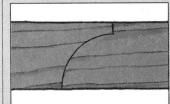 

FINGER GLUE JOINT

To join boards edge to edge and end to end. Similar to glue joint, but offers much more gluing surface.

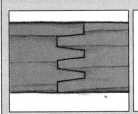 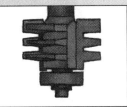

STILE-AND-RAIL JOINT

To join shaped surfaces of frame members that will hold wooden panels. Often used in making cabinet doors.

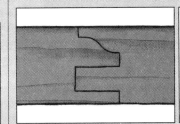 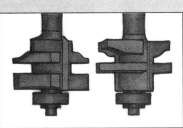

LOCKED MITER JOINT

To make strong 90-degree mitered corners.

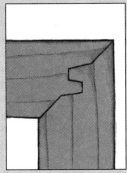 

SASH JOINT

To join the shaped surfaces of "sash work" — frames that will hold glass panels, such as windows and glazed cabinet doors. Similar to stile-and-rail joint, but sticking portion of this joint has rabbet to hold glass rather than groove to hold wooden panel.

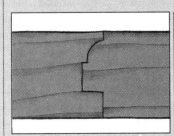 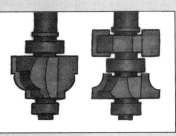

COMMON JIG AND FIXTURE ASSEMBLIES

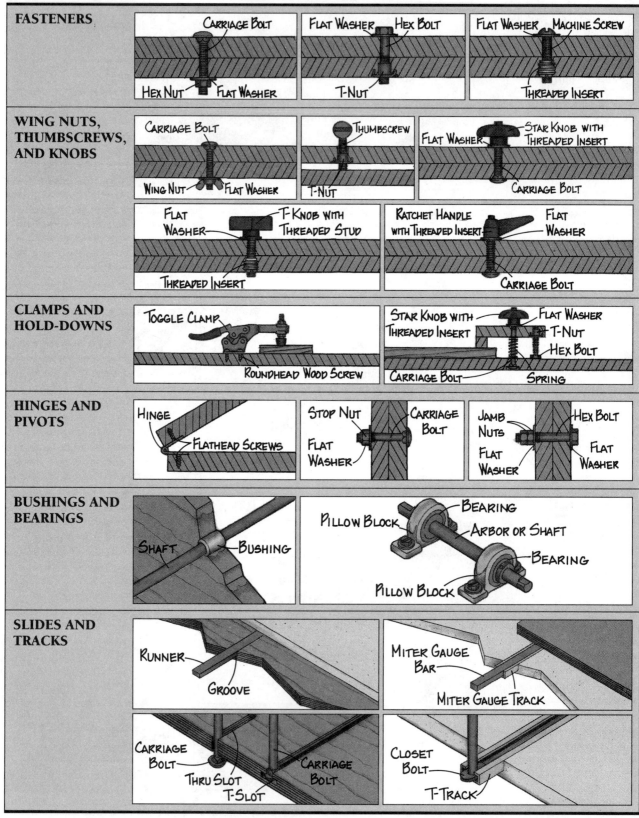

FASTENERS

CARRIAGE BOLT · HEX NUT · FLAT WASHER

FLAT WASHER · HEX BOLT · T-NUT

FLAT WASHER · MACHINE SCREW · THREADED INSERT

WING NUTS, THUMBSCREWS, AND KNOBS

CARRIAGE BOLT · WING NUT · FLAT WASHER

THUMBSCREW · T-NUT

FLAT WASHER · STAR KNOB WITH THREADED INSERT · CARRIAGE BOLT

FLAT WASHER · T-KNOB WITH THREADED STUD · THREADED INSERT

RATCHET HANDLE WITH THREADED INSERT · FLAT WASHER · CARRIAGE BOLT

CLAMPS AND HOLD-DOWNS

TOGGLE CLAMP · ROUNDHEAD WOOD SCREW

STAR KNOB WITH THREADED INSERT · FLAT WASHER · T-NUT · HEX BOLT · CARRIAGE BOLT · SPRING

HINGES AND PIVOTS

HINGE · FLATHEAD SCREWS

STOP NUT · CARRIAGE BOLT · FLAT WASHER

JAMB NUTS · HEX BOLT · FLAT WASHER · FLAT WASHER

BUSHINGS AND BEARINGS

SHAFT · BUSHING

PILLOW BLOCK · BEARING · ARBOR OR SHAFT · BEARING · PILLOW BLOCK

SLIDES AND TRACKS

RUNNER · GROOVE

MITER GAUGE BAR · MITER GAUGE TRACK

CARRIAGE BOLT · THRU SLOT · T-SLOT · CARRIAGE BOLT

CLOSET BOLT · T-TRACK

Jig-Making Materials

MATERIAL	STRENGTH	DURABILITY	STABILITY	SPECIAL PROPERTIES	COMMON USES
WOOD					
Domestic hardwoods (maple, birch, ash, poplar)	High along the grain	High	Low across the grain	Strong and stable along the wood grain; machines easily	Structural parts that require strength and stability in one direction only
Exotic imports (rosewood, cocobolo, bocote, teak)	High along the grain	Very high	Medium across the grain	Strong and stable along the wood grain; decorative; water resistant	Handles, grips, knobs, other frequently handled parts
PLYWOOD					
Hardwood plywood	Medium	Medium-high	Medium	Thin face veneers	Structural parts
European plywood	Medium-high	High	Medium-high	Thick face veneers; easy to machine	Parts requiring extra strength or stability
PARTICLEBOARD					
1-M-2 particleboard	Low	Medium	Medium	Chips easily; difficult to machine	Templates, forms, patterns, work surfaces
Tempered hardboard	Low	Medium-high	High	Hard surface; limited thicknesses	Templates, inserts
Medium-density fiberboard	Low	Medium	High	Easy to machine; remains flat	Templates, forms, patterns, work surfaces
PLASTICS					
Acrylics	Medium	High	Very high	Rigid; available in clear or opaque sheets	Patterns, guards, mounting plates
Polycarbonates	Medium	High	Very high	Flexible; available in clear or opaque sheets	Patterns, guards
UHMW	Medium	Very high	Very high	Flexible; slippery; long-wearing; easy to machine	Runners, guides, moving parts
Phenolics	Medium	Very high	Very high	Rigid; long-wearing	Runners, parts that must not flex
Plastic laminates	Low	High	Very high	Available in thin sheets only	Covering for work surfaces and fences

THE WORKSHOP COMPANION SERIES

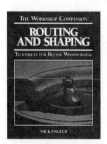

ROUTING AND SHAPING

This is a complete guide to dozens of routing and shaping techniques, including shaped joints and decorative shaping.

HARDCOVER $19.95   ISBN 0-87596-107-X
PAPERBACK $12.95   ISBN 0-87596-610-1

JOINING WOOD

This book takes the mystery out of even complex joints, like the dovetail, splined miter, and mortise and tenon, by showing how all joints are based on five simple cuts.

HARDCOVER $19.95   ISBN 0-87596-121-5

USING THE TABLE SAW

This book covers all the vital basics of the table saw, then shows you special techniques like raising panels, tapering, and cutting coves.

HARDCOVER $19.95   ISBN 0-87596-127-4
PAPERBACK $12.95   ISBN 0-87596-609-8

FINISHING

This book demystifies finishing by breaking it down into three steps: choosing the right finish, preparing the surface, and applying the finish.

HARDCOVER $19.95   ISBN 0-87596-138-X

MAKING BUILT-IN CABINETS

With the techniques shown in this book, you can make entertainment centers, storage units, even an entire set of kitchen cabinets.

HARDCOVER $19.95   ISBN 0-87596-139-8

USING THE BAND SAW

This book shows you how to fine-tune your band saw, make freehand and guided cuts, and resaw thick stock. Special techniques include compound cuts and dovetail cuts.

HARDCOVER $19.95   ISBN 0-87596-140-1

ADVANCED ROUTING

An answer book for the experienced woodworker and a guide for the beginner, this book extends readers' router skills.

HARDCOVER $19.95   ISBN 0-87596-578-4

WORKBENCHES AND SHOP FURNITURE

From benches and vises to mobile tool carts and wood storage racks, this book shows you how to outfit your shop intelligently.

HARDCOVER $19.95   ISBN 0-87596-579-2

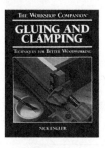

GLUING AND CLAMPING

This is a comprehensive guide to the assembly process, including choosing the right glue and the right clamps. Plus you get plans for 12 shop-made clamps.

HARDCOVER $19.95   ISBN 0-87596-580-6

MAKING DESKS AND BOOKCASES

Learn to design and make classically styled desks and bookcases with shelves that don't sag. Details show how to build for today's electronic and computer equipment.

HARDCOVER $19.95   ISBN 0-87596-581-4

SANDING AND PLANING

See why sanding makes all the difference in the quality of your finished projects, and learn how to use planes like an expert.

HARDCOVER $19.95 ISBN 0-87596-582-2

MAKING TABLES AND CHAIRS

Tackle the challenges of designing and making tables and chairs. This book includes design standards and innovative chairmaking jigs.

HARDCOVER $19.95 ISBN 0-87596-665-1

SHARPENING

This book proves there's no mystery to getting tools perfectly sharp—if you use the right technique and the right guide for each tool.

HARDCOVER $19.95 ISBN 0-87596-584-9

USING HAND TOOLS

Discover the finer points of measuring and marking tools, chisels, planes, and scrapers. And learn how to make hand tools that are better than ones you can buy.

HARDCOVER $19.95 ISBN 0-87596-680-2

MAKING BOXES AND CHESTS

This book develops a system of joinery and construction based on the fact that any furniture project can be reduced to the simple box.

HARDCOVER $19.95 ISBN 0-87596-585-7

USING THE DRILL PRESS

Learn how to choose the right speed and the best bits for your drill press; drill cross grain and end grain, metal, and plastic; and how to sand or grind on the drill press.

HARDCOVER $19.95 ISBN 0-87596-721-3

USING THE SCROLL SAW

This book covers everything you need to know about using the scroll saw—choosing one, adjustments, materials, marquetry, intarsia, and inlay techniques.

HARDCOVER $19.95 ISBN 0-87596-654-3

MAKING JIGS AND FIXTURES

Increase the versatility of every tool in your shop with this detailed guide, including plans for 12 essential jigs.

HARDCOVER $19.95 ISBN 0-87596-689-6

FINISH CARPENTRY

Discover professional techniques for installing doors, windows, wood floors, wainscoting, and trim. Plans include stained glass windows, a paneled door, and a coffered ceiling.

HARDCOVER $19.95 ISBN 0-87596-583-0

WOOD AND WOODWORKING MATERIALS

Learn about lumbering techniques, moisture content, wood defects, veneer, plywood, and particleboard.

HARDCOVER $19.95 ISBN 0-87596-722-1

To order any of these books, call 1-800-527-8200.

WOODWORKING GLOSSARY

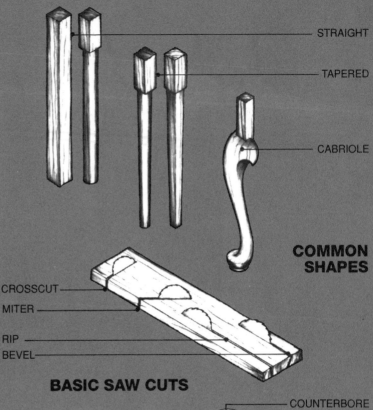

STRAIGHT

TAPERED

CABRIOLE

COMMON SHAPES

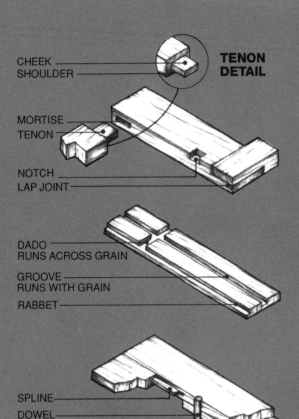

CHEEK
SHOULDER

TENON DETAIL

MORTISE
TENON

NOTCH
LAP JOINT

DADO
RUNS ACROSS GRAIN

GROOVE
RUNS WITH GRAIN

RABBET

SPLINE
DOWEL
GLUE BLOCK

BASIC JOINERY

CROSSCUT
MITER
RIP
BEVEL

BASIC SAW CUTS

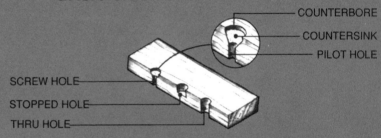

COUNTERBORE
COUNTERSINK
PILOT HOLE

SCREW HOLE
STOPPED HOLE
THRU HOLE

HOLES

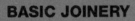

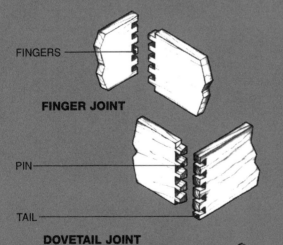

FINGERS

FINGER JOINT

PIN

TAIL

DOVETAIL JOINT

BLIND DADO

BLIND RABBET

SPECIAL JOINERY

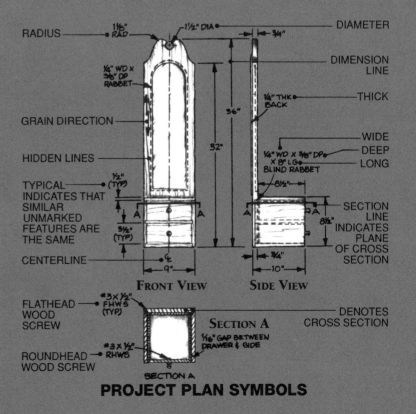

RADIUS

1½" RAD

1½" DIA

¾"

DIAMETER

¼" WD x ⅜" DP RABBET

36"

¼" THK BACK

DIMENSION LINE

THICK

GRAIN DIRECTION

32"

WIDE
¼" WD x ⅜" DP x 8" LG BLIND RABBET

DEEP
LONG

HIDDEN LINES

TYPICAL INDICATES THAT SIMILAR UNMARKED FEATURES ARE THE SAME

½" (TYP)

8½"

A   A

A

A

SECTION LINE INDICATES PLANE OF CROSS SECTION

9½" (TYP)

8½"

CENTERLINE

¢
9"

¾"
10"

FRONT VIEW   **SIDE VIEW**

FLATHEAD WOOD SCREW

#3 X ½" FHWS (TYP)

ROUNDHEAD WOOD SCREW

#3 X ½" RHWS

Section A

1/16" GAP BETWEEN DRAWER & SIDE

SECTION A

DENOTES CROSS SECTION

PROJECT PLAN SYMBOLS